GRACE IN TRANSITION

The First Four Seasons

GRACE IN TRANSITION
The First Four Seasons

CASSANDRA GRACE

gatekeeper press™

Columbus, Ohio

Grace in Transition: The First Four Seasons

Published by Gatekeeper Press
2167 Stringtown Rd, Suite 109
Columbus, OH 43123-2989
www.GatekeeperPress.com

ISBN (hardcover): 9781662907104
ISBN (paperback): 9781662907111
eISBN: 9781662907128

To everyone crossing the bridge of fear as they head toward change, and to all those who lend support along the way.

GRACE IN TRANSITION

THE FIRST FOUR SEASONS

WELCOME

Early in my transition I used to hate hearing "You're so brave!" in response to anything I did. I know it was well-meaning and I took it in stride because I knew it was this person's way of engaging with me in a civil way. All things being equal, I vastly prefer "You're so brave" to "You look ridiculous, you freak." But after a while it started to really bother me.

For starters, I resented being told that being myself was somehow "brave." Like, me going to Trader Joe's in a sundress to stock up on prosecco should not be perceived as "brave." It should be perceived as "Tuesday."

Then I started to think about it a little deeper and it began to bother me a little more. Are you calling me brave because I am not actually pulling this look off as well as I think I am? Are you calling me brave the way someone who tries and fails at something is called brave? Are you giving me a participation prize? I am not the kind of person who expects a trophy for just showing up, so please take your "Everyone is an All-Star!" condescension elsewhere.

Those were my initial knee-jerk reactions to all the lovely people who were extending me kindness as I took my first awkward steps into the world presenting as myself. More jerk than knee, I know. Estrogen only does so much. I have a lifetime of occasionally being a dick, let alone having one, to unpack and process.

As I worked on this book, though, I've developed a bit of a different perspective. Looking at where I was in my presentation when I first put my story online, thinking about where my head was at then compared to where it is at now, well, I've definitely come to the conclusion: yeah, that was pretty brave.

Which brings us to this book and how it came about.

It all basically started with an email that I wrote to Sephora in the summer of 2019. I am presenting it here in full as it does a solid job of setting the stage for what is to come:

How Eyeshadow Changed My Life—A Transgender Woman's Experience at Sephora

Greetings! My name is Cassandra Grace and I am a middle-aged, late-blooming transgender woman. I would like to share with you what an incredibly positive, supportive, life-affirming role the Sephora staff in Reston, VA, has played for me and my transition. This is going to be long, so get some popcorn—it will be worth it.

First of all, I want to stress up front that the 'middle-aged, late-blooming' thing is kind of an important part of this story. I know that Sephora runs a very, very inclusive ship and that all the colors of the rainbow are welcome at your amazing stores. I'm sharing this story only because I know that now, after experiencing this for myself.

For most of my life, however, I had no idea that I was welcome, not just in your stores but in the world in general. And by the way things are looking, with the coordinated effort to roll back hard-won rights and freedoms currently underway, there is no guarantee going forward that many of us who proudly call that rainbow home are going to be as welcome, let alone tolerated, as we currently are.

What I'm about to share, though, is a Good News story. If you find it compelling, then I ask you to share it with as many people as you can to help push back against all the Bad News stories that seem to be gathering in strength.

I'm 47 years old. I've known since I was a young child that something was seriously off about my body, but I didn't know what, so roughly the first forty or so of my years were a total cluster. I didn't even really know how much of a cluster because the broader awareness of transgender issues that only very recently has emerged simply did not exist back then. So I suffered and did the only thing that made sense to me, which was try and be the most alpha, confident, manly man I could be in order to overcome the mistake of my existence.

Around two years ago, though, I reached a point where I couldn't do it anymore. I did everything I thought I needed to do to fit into society's expectations for me and none of it was working. Thanks to the Internet and the many personal stories of their own painful journeys that so many transgender people were openly sharing, however, I started to understand what this thing was that had been haunting me my entire life. I also started to believe that I could do something about it.

After consulting with all the appropriate medical professionals—a privilege not everyone in my situation has, by the way—I decided to start a course of low-dose hormones to see if it would at least quiet the awful tension in my head that was causing me so much pain. I did not plan on transitioning and I did not think that I would ever be in a position to do so. Too old. Too masculine. Too much baggage. All I wanted was to quiet the noise and see if I could live out the rest of my life with less pain.

Almost immediately I felt better. Calmer. More balanced. Less tension between mind and body. And then, as a few months passed, other changes started to happen. Skin, body hair, fat distribution—everything started changing. Little by little, as I very slowly reduced the testosterone in my body and very slowly replaced it with estrogen, my body started to look and feel the way my mind always knew it should.

And then the craziest freaking thing happened.

I have hated having my picture taken my entire life. Hated it. Never smiled, never liked what I saw after the picture was taken, just hated it. About four months into low-dose hormones, though, I was lying in bed one morning and feeling pretty chill so I decided to take a selfie. I was curious to see if I looked the way I felt. I snapped the pic, pulled it up, and started crying. Not just crying but sobbing. What I saw that morning was something I had never, ever seen before: myself. That was the first picture I had ever taken where I looked at it and saw myself.

That moment marked a turning point in my faith that Hormone Replacement Therapy was right for me. Throughout the rest of 2018 I slowly increased my dosage and prepared the groundwork for something I thought I would never be in a position to do: transition and live my life openly as the woman I've always been. By early 2019 I had gathered enough confidence and my body had changed in so many wonderful, affirming ways that I decided to go for it. Prior to this I had only been transitioning medically, i.e. taking hormones. To the outside world I was still presenting as a man, although a pretty slender one with really good skin and a surprising capacity to listen. But a man, nonetheless.

All this sounds great and positive and affirming and all that, but I have to tell you that it was terrifying AF. Every single step of this process has been terrifying before I've taken it. Every one. So the fear and anxiety and doubt that I experienced when I walked into the Reston Sephora back in February of this year (we finally got to the good, Sephora-related part of the story—thanks for your patience!!) was overwhelming. I had walked past many times before, never having the courage to go in. This time, though, this time was going to be different.

I had no idea what I was doing. I had no idea what was possible. I had no idea if I would be laughed at or turned away. I just knew that I had to do something about my horrible ignorance concerning makeup and skincare if I was going to finally step out into the world as me.

I walked in, went up to someone who looked like she knew what she was doing, and asked if I could get some help. I explained my deal and before I knew it—not fully conscious of what was happening because of how freaking scared I still was—I was sitting in a chair in front of a massive mirror in the middle of a store filled with women getting a mini tutorial on eye shadow.

Then we moved on to mascara.

The woman who helped me that evening—Lucy—gave me something that I had never had before: the experience of a stranger respecting and treating me seriously as a woman. All of the staff at the Reston store have been unfailingly nice to me in the months that have since passed, and I've even become friends with some of them. It was Lucy, though, and her example of inclusivity and acceptance that has literally changed my life.

I never had the experience of learning from my mother's example or experimenting with various techniques with my girlfriends growing up. I never saw anyone on TV or in a magazine who I could look up to and say to myself 'I can look like that.' I only saw unattainable ideals that I'd be cruelly kept from emulating because of the mistake of my birth.

Lucy showed me that night that I wasn't a mistake. That I had potential. That I had natural features that I could highlight instead of cover up, that I could draw attention to myself for all the right reasons and not all the wrong ones.

I cannot overstate how important this was to me and how differently things could have developed if my experience had been less positive.

It's been six months now and I pop into the Reston store about once a week. Ok...maybe a couple times a week. :) Everyone at the store has been amazingly supportive as I've gained confidence in my presentation—I just recently discovered the magic of bold eyebrows!!—and it's been a joy for me to share with them my experience of emerging into the world as myself.

I made Rouge status not too long ago and in what I consider to be the ultimate celebration of my transition, I treated myself to a VIP ticket to the Sephoria House of Beauty in early September. Yes, I just wrote that. I've gone from being terrified to step into your store earlier this year to booking a trip to Los Angeles to attend this amazing celebration of beauty culture you are holding next month.

I would love for you to somehow recognize the incredible contribution the Reston store, and Lucy in particular, has made to my life. Additionally, I imagine you get lots of positive testimonials, but if you think mine is worth sharing more broadly, I would be honored for this story to be circulated among a broader community.

I'd also happily share a cocktail with any of you who are reading this in the VIP Lounge next month. :)

Please keep doing what you are doing—it changes lives. It changed mine and I am very, very grateful to everyone involved. Thank you.

I wrote that in July of 2019. I sent it to the manager of my local Sephora store as well as to the Regional Manager. Within a few weeks I was in touch with Sephora Corporate about meeting some of their executives on my trip to LA. Come September, I indeed sat down and shared cocktails with some of them in the VIP Lounge where we discussed ways to share my story more broadly.

Shortly after hitting send on that email to Sephora I also wrote a lengthy message of appreciation to Anthropologie, the swanky boho-chic clothing chain with the awesome-smelling candles. There is an Anthropologie right across the street from my local Sephora, and not long after I got my eye shadow tutorial, I went in and asked to try on clothes. It was the first time I had ever been in a women's clothing store and like my experience with Sephora, I was treated with decency, kindness, and complete respect for my identity.

One thing to keep in mind here is that at the time there was NOTHING about my outward appearance that tracked with the conventional customer base of either store. Less euphemistically, I was still heavily on the "dude" end of the gender-presentation spectrum. Granted, Sephora is very progressive, has been for some time, and is forward-leaning in catering to a very broad demographic. Anthropologie, on the other hand, is one of those places that has a more specific clientele, and if all you did was look at me when I stepped into that store, I was not it.

To my great surprise, though, I was welcomed with open arms and I felt seen in a way that was very new for me. This unconditional acceptance gave me the confidence boost I needed to take the next step towards a full medical and social transition.

Furthermore, both experiences were formative in the series of fortunate events that led me to start my Instagram. For example, that chat with Sephora execs led to my participation in their "We Belong to Something Beautiful" campaign. Anthropologie responded to my expressions of gratitude by inviting me to film a training video for their staff and walk the runway in their September 2019 Fall Fashion Show at their Georgetown location. And that was just the beginning.

But it was those two experiences—the Sephora campaign and walking a runway for Anthropologie—that kicked things off.

Prior to October 2019 I had never been on social media in any capacity. Ever. No Facebook, no Twitter. Nope, not even GeoCities or Myspace. I just never understood what the appeal was. Aside from that, there was nothing about myself that I wanted to share. It's similar to why the vast majority of my pre-transition photos all have that same "I don't want my picture taken" expression.

Similarly, as much as I had tried over the years, I was never able to keep a diary. Every time I tried to start one, I became very conscious that I didn't know who the intended audience was. I know, right? You write a diary to yourself! But when the "yourself" part of the equation isn't in focus, the whole purpose of a diary kind of breaks down. At least it did for me.

As I mentioned in that email to Sephora, one of the earliest markers of my transition being a positive development was that I started taking selfies. I truly HATED having my picture taken prior to beginning HRT, but that first moment when I looked at my phone screen and recognized myself was like a dam bursting. I started obsessively taking photos and for the first time in my life, I was proud of what I saw.

I still had no desire to share my photos with strangers, though, much less take a photo of what I had for lunch and release that valuable piece of content into the world. That's pretty much what I thought Instagram was: "here's what I had for lunch: behold."

As I have come to learn, that was a not entirely faulty assumption.

Anyway, I knew that the Sephora video would be posted on Instagram, so I decided to get on that platform, primarily to be able to watch the video. And to see what kind of reaction there would be to it. My very first post? A photo of me walking the runway during the Anthropologie show.

A few weeks later the Sephora video dropped, and while it did not catapult me to viral fame, it did teach me a valuable lesson about engaging with strangers online. As the weeks passed, I began to appreciate what an incredible sandbox Instagram represented for me to find and hone my voice. I started to pay more attention to the kinds of photos I was posting, engage with others in a substantive way, and as people responded positively, share more introspective reflections about my journey.

Before long I realized that I was using Instagram as the diary I never had. Every new milestone, every new realization, many of the events that made up my daily life—I found a way to document my transition in a way that was meaningful to me. Moreover, it was meaningful enough to others who routinely responded to the chronicle of my unfolding adventures with appreciation, encouragement, and a sense of real community.

Another thing that I realized early in my Instagramming was that one day I would use the material I was sharing in some project, most likely a book. My experiences with Sephora and Anthropologie and my connection with people on an individual level had made it clear to me that there was some power in my story, something that people were connecting with. I didn't fully understand what it was—especially as I was still discovering so many things about myself as I stepped more and more openly into the world—but I knew that something was going on.

The idea for a book started to come together in the Autumn of 2020. As I began to review my posts—really looking at them with some measure of distance and perspective for the first time—I was struck by how neatly clear narrative arcs began to come into focus. This was not by design. In other words, it's not like I was artificially creating situations as part of some "Cassandra Cinematic Universe" Master Plan. I was just doing my thing, documenting it as I went along, and what you see here is what happened over the course of a year *as* it happened.

The conceit of arranging everything as if it were a scripted series is a story that I tell later in the book, so I want to leave it there as it is anchored to a specific moment in time. When that idea came to me, though, it was kind of wild to see how everything just fell into place Tetris-like into well-defined seasons with distinct storylines.

I look back at those first few posts and I see an awkward, gangly teenager just beginning puberty. Then I see a young woman finding her footing, filled with excitement at the prospect of stepping out into the world. I see hopes dashed, lessons learned, and renewed purpose take flight. Finally, as the events covered in the latter part of the book draw closer to the time that I am writing these words, I see someone who is finally right where she needs to be.

As of this writing, I have 375 posts on Instagram. Close to one a day over the past year or so. The 65 that I present here tell a very specific story, the one that I want to share with you. It is the story of my effort to make up for lost time—lost decades, in fact—and live as fully, richly, authentically, and purposefully as possible in appreciation for the gift of reincarnation that my gender transition represents.

As far as the other 300 or so posts, there are a LOT of "storylines" that I didn't cover here, a lot of content that I am really proud of that just didn't fit with the purpose of this book. That you purchased this book means a lot to me and I hope you find it worth your time and money. If you do, by all means check out the Bonus Content waiting for you on my still-hopping Insta.

The posts are presented in chronological order as they happened. The only editing that has been done is to remove references to specific people and the occasional extraneous word. I have also not gone back and edited the posts that are up on Instagram.

As far as the photos that I am sharing, I did hire a very gifted creator who I met on Instagram to try and squeeze every last bit of quality out of them. All of the photos were taken with my iPhone 7 selfie camera and I wanted to see what she could do in terms of lighting and clarity of image. I am as militant about the authenticity of my photos as I am with my words, though, so that means no photoshopping, no airbrushing, no filters that change my appearance in any way.

I want to make explicitly clear, like ALL CAPS EXPLICITLY CLEAR, that what I am sharing here is my experience and my experience alone. I am not speaking on behalf of anyone else and not claiming that my experience is representative of anyone else's, whether they are trans or not. All opinions in here are my own, all definitions are mine, all perspectives radiate from my sole vantage point.

However, I very much hope that you find this book compelling. Whoever you are, whatever your deal, wherever you are headed in life, I hope you find some relevance here to your own journey, some relatable lessons about the power of kindness, compassion, and empathy. Our world would be a better place if we all took it upon ourselves to create more opportunities for others to live their truth so that we can more easily live our own.

I hope you find the book so compelling that you tell everyone in your social network about it and encourage them to buy it. Honestly, hardcover, paperback, or ebook—the royalties are pretty much the same whatever version—so do what's best for you and the ten friends you need gifts for.

Before you dive into the book, though, I would like to acknowledge something.

I believe very strongly that beauty is in the eye of the beholder, that art is open to every possible interpretation and all that good stuff. I hope that a substantial number of people—hundreds of thousands would be a nice start—find the content in this book compelling, that it speaks to them on any number of possible levels. I know the levels I would like it to speak to you on, and if it does tickle any fancies or inspire some purposeful self-reflection about the course of your life, I'd love to hear from you! My DMs are always open.

I would also like to go on record up front that someone dismissing the book as delusional narcissistic self-absorption will not come as a surprise to me. That is a totally valid takeaway from a certain point of view and if those words find their way into the title of the New York Times review, so be it. "*Grace In Transition: The First Four Seasons, An Exercise in Delusional Narcissistic Self-Absorption*" has a certain ring to it and if it drives sales, I'm not going to complain.

As the Poetess notes, haters gonna hate, hate, hate, hate, hate. And the idea that someone thinks their Instagram posts are worthy of book treatment does have an air of, well, shall we say: "Are you fucking kidding me?" about it.

In my mind, however, this is not a book about a trans woman's Instagram account any more than Siddhartha was about a rootless dude with a ton of privilege. I mean, those are admittedly the lead characters, but that's not really what either of these books is about.

Yes, I just placed this book in the same sentence as Siddhartha. As I mentioned, I am quite aware of the potential charge of "delusional narcissistic self-absorption" and I decided to lean into it as hard as I can.

Here is where you will find the photograph that accompanied the original Instagram post. This is an artist's rendering of one of the photos appearing in Season Four.

SAMPLE EPISODE | Cassandra Explains the Format of the Book

Dear Reader:

This book is presented as a companion to the content I have shared on my Instagram, as if that content were an award-winning series on a streaming service.

Trust me, it's going to make sense.

The "episodes" in each season represent posts that appeared on my Instagram, to include the photo I used and any accompanying language. That language— along with a few of the hashtags from the original post—is presented here in these boxes in italicized font.

Instead of binge-watching, you will "binge-read" a show about a middle- aged trans woman finding her way in the world, her path illuminated by the kindness of others.

That's the concept, and I hope you have as much fun experiencing it as I did in creating it for you.

Spoiler Alert: I had a lot of fun creating it.

#spellingitout #tellyourfriends
#perfectgift #betterthanbitcoin
#leavenothingtochance

The majority of the content in this book is presented in this section.

Sometimes I'll offer up a continuation of the action referenced in the Original Post.

Sometimes you'll find a bit of "Behind the Scenes" insight into other stuff going on.

Very rarely, however, do I let you just enjoy the majesty of the Instagram content on its own.

What I'm trying to say is that I didn't just cut and paste stuff that I already posted on Instagram.

Like, I actually wrote a book.

—Cassandra

SEASON ONE

GIRL MEETS WORLD

S1E1 | Cassandra Walks A Runway

I've been told that I need to have an Instagram by my incredibly multi-talented daughter, so I'm going to listen to her.

This picture was from the Anthropologie Fall Fashion Show in Georgetown, where I lived out a dream on top of a dream with another dream shoved in there for good measure.

#thisiswhattranslookslike #runway

#positiveenergy #anthropologie

At the time, this all felt like a kind of Victory Lap to mark the tremendous effort it had taken to get to this point, a triumphant celebration of my transition as a mission satisfyingly accomplished. I had gone further than I ever really expected to go, was regularly accepted by others—complete strangers, even—as a woman, and so the "transition" part was done, right? I mean, I was even walking in a freaking fashion show!

Looking back from the vantage point of now, however, I clearly see how this was more of a beginning than an end, a true Debutante's Ball marking the first page of the next volume of my life. I now realize that whatever I achieve, whatever milestones are marked, my transition will never really have an end. It is an ongoing process filled with unexpected twists and turns and constantly expanding horizons, an outlook I have come to fully embrace.

This has helped me manage some of the things that have not turned out the way I had hoped as well as appreciate all the things that I never dreamed of happening in the first place. In other words, my transition has become synonymous with my life. It is not a process separate from it.

One other thing about looking at this photo now is that I see nothing particularly feminine about my appearance. I mean, the hair, the earrings, the dress...fine. While the dress is admittedly rather feminine, the person wearing it? Yeah, not so much.

I look at that photo and I am filled with gratitude for the fact that I was accepted and embraced as a woman by everyone at that event, from the organizers, to the other women who walked the runway, to everyone in the crowd. However I actually looked—and hey, let's be honest, the stylist did an amazing job with my hair—people were responding to my radiant energy more than anything else.

Until a winner emerges from the Netflix/HBO Max bidding war that is about to happen, the best movie yet to be made about my transition is Amy Schumer's 'I Feel Pretty'. Hear me out. When she falls off the exercise bike, hits her head, and is suddenly convinced that she is the hottest thing to ever walk this planet, well, that is EXACTLY what I felt like during this time.

I swear to you, watching her glide through the world with zero effs to give about what anyone else thinks was a revelation. That was the attitude that I embraced when I decided to finally step out into the world as myself and you can really see that here.

That said, as I mentioned in the introduction, I do look back at these photos and I have a much better appreciation for why everyone was telling me how brave I was.

S1E2 | Cassandra Would Really, Really Love to Stick Around

I think there's something you should know

I think it's time I stopped the show

There's something deep inside of me

There's someone I forgot to be

Take back your picture in a frame

Don't think that I'll be back again

I just hope you understand

Sometimes the clothes do not make the man.

#thisiswhattranslookslike #runway
#positiveenergy #anthropologie

I stepped into an Anthropologie store to buy clothes for the first time in February, 2019 and I was a sweaty, nervous, fearful mess. I went back a few weeks later, and while it wasn't exactly a walk in the park, it had become a little easier.

Then other ladies started giving me compliments—"God, I wish I had your legs" was a common one—and it got a little easier. This photo captures the moment when it stopped getting easier and just "was."

Freedom, indeed.

This photo represents the pure joy that I experienced from shedding the last bits of guilt, shame, and self-consciousness I had about being in a women's dressing room.

For those not hip to the reference, the lyrics are from George Michael's anthem of liberation.

S1E3

Two years. There is a lot going on here but if a picture tells a thousand words then I'm going to just let these two do most of the talking. For context, though, that picture on the left was me two years ago right as I was starting to come to terms with being trans and thinking about what, if anything, I could do about it given how old and masculine and spent I felt.

I've known since I was about six that I was in the wrong body and I spent the following forty years assuming there was nothing I could do about it. Like many assumptions people make about the potential for change I was so, so wrong. But I just didn't know better, so I suffered in ignorance and along the way caused other people to suffer because of how deeply unhappy and unsatisfied and hopeless I felt at my core.

To the actual very few people who loved me anyway and supported and stuck with me as I finally figured this all out: thank you for seeing me underneath all the pain. To the many, many more people who only know me as the radiantly happy creature on the right: thank you for all the love and support you give me each and every day that helps me focus on all that I've gained and learned as I navigate this journey.

#betterlatethannever #hrt

#transitiontuesday

#alwaysmovingforward

Cassandra Experiences Double Vision for the First Time

Every Tuesday on Instagram, many trans people from around the world post "Then and Now" photos to visually represent the progress they have made. This was the first #transitiontuesday photo I ever posted and like many "firsts" this one was terrifying. Lots of reasons, but the primary one is that I want people to accept me for the woman I am, not the man I looked like. That is a very, very loaded sentence and I would need to write another book to really unpack all the complexity going on there. Bottom line for those who aren't trans: when you feel what is visible on the right, the last thing you want is a reminder of what is visible on the left.

These photos, though, serve many useful purposes. They are an obvious marker of change and a visually compelling explanation for why someone embarks on a transition. There is a reason why we do this, and that reason is visible in both photos. Additionally, for many of us, especially those like me who are up there in years, we grapple with tremendous fear and uncertainty over whether it's even worth it, whether or not it's simply too late.

Photos like these—of middle-aged trans women documenting their progress online—gave me hope that something could be salvaged of my life by transitioning. As painful as it sometimes is to look back at what was, I continue to put photos like these out there to help inspire others think about what can still be.

S1E4 | Cassandra Experiences Resting Model Face

This was my homage to the classic boardgame Clue. Colonel Mustard on the staircase with a sick lewk. Get it? I realize that joke appeals to the very narrow demographic of fashionista boardgame aficionados, but for the three of you out there: you're welcome.

Literally the only reason why I included this post is because I like that joke so much. Wait a minute. I meant to say in-Clue-ded.

I feel like I'm making progress on my Resting Model Face since the Anthropologie show.

One minor slip-up at the end, though.

#transmodel #whynotme

#wheresmymodellingcontract

#hrt #legsfordays

S1E5 | Cassandra Dresses Up Like A Girl

'Dress up like a girl.' I remember doing that for Halloween in fifth grade. Didn't really know why it felt so free, so liberating, but I remember it was the last time for close to forty years I'd feel that lack of shame.

All the 'putting on women's clothes' that took place over that time—all of it behind closed doors—was fraught with shame and confusion and guilt.

And then I stopped 'putting on women's clothes' and I started to wear clothes. I stopped 'dressing up' and started dressing. Now I just am. As free and happy and without guilt or shame as a child. Literally shame-less. No more costumes. This is me.

#betterlatethannever #hrt #transition-tuesday #alwaysmovingforward

As you will see as these seasons unfold, my fashion sense has undergone something of an evolution. And thank goodness for that, because I don't know what the heck I was thinking with this outfit. Ok, ok, I actually do know. I remember thinking that this outfit was the absolute height of fashion. Not only that, but I also thought my makeup here was ON POINT.

Early in my transition, one of my trans mentors told me something about taking photos that really stuck with me. She said, "As you transition, every photo you take is both the best photo you've ever taken and the worst photo you've ever taken." I remember sitting there smiling and nodding and thinking this was the most mysterious Yoda shit I had ever heard. Like, WTF did that even mean?

With time, though, I came to appreciate how wisely and succinctly she described something that I have repeatedly experienced ever since.

You take a photo—like this one for example—and in the moment you compare it with how you looked before. The general reaction is "OMG I LOOK SO BEAUTIFUL I CAN'T BELIEVE ALL THIS IS HAPPENING!" Then you share this photo with friends, or put it on social media, or order a big banner from Costco and hang it in your bedroom. It is literally the best photo you have ever taken. Up to that point.

You keep doing this day after day after day, and every day you have a new "OMG THIS IS THE BEST PHOTO EVER" moment. Then one day you are scrolling through your photos or looking at your post history and you see something from six months ago. At which point you say to yourself: "OMG HOW COULD I HAVE SHARED THIS HIDEOUS PHOTO WITH THE WORLD I'M SO DISGUSTING."

The moment this becomes an actual problem requiring therapy is when you start to wonder whether ANY of your photos are good. The brain goes: "Well, you thought that earlier photo was amazing and now you realize it was crap. You may think you look pretty good today, but the odds are in favor of you looking back six months from now and realizing this photo is crap as well. Ipso facto you're a monster and you should never show your face in public again." Something like that.

I'm assuming this is what Middle School was like for most of you. I wouldn't exactly know, because I repressed my entire first puberty as a coping mechanism. I mean that very literally. That whole experience of having a male body develop around me was so deeply traumatic in ways that I had zero capability to understand that I basically blacked it all out as it was happening.

As a result, this second physical puberty that I have induced as part of my Hormone Replacement Therapy is in many respects my first real emotional puberty. And I'm doing it as I approach 50! How exciting is that?!

S1E6 | Cassandra Belongs to Something Beautiful

As some of you may know, I was featured in a Sephora campaign last week. (Really, Cassandra, I had NO IDEA based on your Instagram) What very few of you know is that the video really effed with my head and caused a massive dysphoric episode that I'm just now pulling out of. Lemme 'splain.

For me, doing this video represented a celebration of how far I've come thanks to the open, accepting, inclusive arms of people like @lucycruzmua . Sephora originally talked about filming the video in San Francisco but I wanted it to be filmed where I live so that Lucy and my local store could be featured, as it's not really just my story, but our story.

I loved the experience of making the video and everyone at Sephora has truly been amazing at every level, every step of the way. This is a massive Good News story! I'm thrilled that the video is out, at the story it tells, at the platform I was given, at all the new people (you!!) who came to my Instagram. It's all good.

But up until last week I had never heard myself talk post-transition. I had never seen myself move. #toomanyselfies . I had never really stopped and reflected on all that really has changed since I walked into that store earlier this year and asked for an eyeshadow tutorial.

Watching the video also took me back to that moment when I reached out for help and that's what triggered the dysphoria and sent me spiraling. But I needed that. I needed to appreciate the journey I've been on and all the people along the way who helped me get to where I am today.

One of the questions I was asked for the video was what I would tell my eleven-year-old self. This wasn't included in the feature, but here is my answer: I would tell her that one day everything will make sense. One day, all the confusion, all the frustration, all the self-loathing will all melt away and you will step into who you were meant to be. I would tell her that the struggle will be worth it, that one day, more and more eleven-year-olds will have the support and love and understanding in place to start living their best lives from the get-go.

I would also tell her that when she hears the name 'Amazon' to buy as many shares of stock as she can and to be patient.

#thisiswhattranslookslike
#bestlife #transandproud

I was very nervous ahead of the posting of this video because I assumed that not everyone who saw it would be all "YOU GO GIRL!!!" in response. I made it a point to stay online as much as I could over the first few days it was out because I wanted to respond to every single comment that was posted, to include what I expected to be a deluge of derision and harassment.

To my great surprise, most comments were supportive and encouraging. There were, however, a few that fell short of "OMG YOU ARE AMAZING THANK YOU FOR SHARING YOUR JOURNEY!!" I saw these, though, as opportunities to engage with people and see if I could show them the person that I am beyond whatever prejudice they may hold.

I am sharing the following exchange word-for-word because, well, see for yourself:

@jbuchalla: This is what happens when you feed your monsters...If this was an antidote for depression, I'd be all over it. Sephora, we just want to see your amazing products stop making this political to get likes.

@grace_in_transition: Hi! Believe me, all I want from Sephora is their amazing products as well. I'm really happy to be able to enjoy them and be part of a broad group of customers who feel welcomed in their store. Whatever you may think of gender dysphoria or any other issue that so many people have to deal with, wouldn't it be great if we could just celebrate everyone having access to the things they need to help them reach their potential?

@jbuchalla: See how sweet of a person you are? Of course you deserve to be celebrated for absolute 100% SURE FACT! You are happy you found your way and that is a BEAUTIFUL priceless accomplishment but as a mom and an entrepreneur I feel that these corporations are just messing up our system using political trends to sell and become popular and that causes misinterpretation and a hype that is planted in a mindless society. Of course I am happy for you and for everyone else who owns it, but being such a huge company like Sephora, they should be neutral to trendy topics! I'm a tired mom, why don't they celebrate me when I shop in their stores? The new generation is in trouble and

we can't ignore that, no matter who you are. Much love for you! I mean it!

@grace_in_transition: Hey @sephora!! Can we please do a "Tired Mom" #webelongtosomethingbeautiful video? Seriously! Think about how this little exchange could have gone off the rails given the way people usually talk to each other on the internet. If you do one, I nominate @jbuchalla! And truly, this warmed MY heart. A little bit of love and compassion—both ways—can do a lot.

@jbuchalla: Never forget what a beautiful person you are.

@grace_in_transition: You too! Tired moms are heroes! I'm so glad this did NOT follow the script. Be well and thank you for this little exchange of kindness.

We remain Instafriends to this day.

S1E7 | Cassandra Is A Danger Behind The Wheel

The driving Selfie. An underappreciated art form, IMHO, although probably for good reason. Most of these were taken at or near a stoplight. I think. Anyway, starting with the top left and working our way down, we're looking at about a year's worth of progress with that one smack dab in the middle taken on my birthday this past May.

I absolutely HATED having my picture taken up until HRT. And then the wildest thing happened: sometime in early 2018, just a few months after starting a very low dose of estrogen, I took a selfie, pulled it up on my phone, and started sobbing.

For the first time in my life I recognized myself in a picture. 46 years in and I finally saw the person who had always been there. The person who the dysphoria had been preventing me from seeing.

10,000 selfies later, I feel like life is just getting going.

Blessings and good vibes to everyone who puts themselves out there each and every day, whether it's Tuesday or not, in the hopes of just being seen, regardless of who you are and where you are in your life.

#thisiswhattranslookslike

#bestlife #transandproud

Wow, I really used to use a lot of product in my hair. Aside from that insightful observation, this is a nice Deep Cut that hints at the material I would use if I ever did *Grace In Transition: The Prequel.*

Fun fact: my formal legal name change to Cassandra Grace was approved by the court on my actual birthday, which is when that photo in the center square was taken.

S1E8 | Cassandra Takes A Step Forward

Nine months ago I walked into an Anthropologie store and tried on clothes for the first time. Nine months ago I made the decision to up my estrogen to a full transition dose. Nine months ago I committed to a social transition.

As my friend who took these pictures today reminded me, nine months is how long it takes someone to be born. This girl is just beginning to take her first steps into the world...

#anthropologie #steppingout #babysteps

#statementpiece #fashionblogger

For those not in the know, gender dysphoria is a distorted self-image that makes you think that nothing has changed and that you still look like you did prior to beginning your transition. That is a simplistic definition for a complex phenomenon, but for the purposes of our discussion here it works just fine. It is something I continue to have to manage and there are still moments—usually once a month for a couple of days—when I will look in the mirror and see "him."

I think I look really cute in this photo, so this isn't about dysphoria, but rather body dysmorphia. As I pulled together photos for this book, one of my Key Takeaways is that I was really, really skinny. Like, too skinny. Like, eating disorder skinny.

I remember thinking at the time how wonderful it was that I could fit into this Size 2 skirt. Yes, you heard that correctly. I thought this was a significant accomplishment. Like a "Suck it, Anne Hathaway in The Devil Wears Prada!!" kind of accomplishment.

As I am beginning to appreciate—but in all honesty am still working on—things got a little out of control on the mind-over-matter front. Not all of the photos that I chose for this book reflect that, but if you go back and look at my Instagram from this time, it's pretty obvious. At least it is to me now, and I'm trying to apply this awareness to develop a healthier self-image going forward.

S1E9 | Cassandra Gets ROMANtic

Now we just need to find an occasion that lets me wear this dress. Target run? Driver's license renewal? Late night Chipotle craving? Something. Anything. What a dress.

A massive "THANK YOU!!" to the wonderful girls at @shopromanusa for their insights and mad photography skillz. I love this freaking dress.

#transmodel #whynotme #hrt

#legsfordays

#wheresmymodellingcontract

Roman is a boutique clothing store in every sense of the word. They only have two locations—one here outside of Washington DC and another in Philadelphia—and their pieces are just...different. My relationship with their clothes and their staff is every bit as meaningful to me and my story as is my connection to multi-national brands like Sephora and Lululemon. Many of the outfits in which I utterly slay are from Roman. In fact, at this point, they are the most-represented brand in my closet.

I could tell story after story about what their clothes mean to me, but I'll let the photos do that work. It's pretty evident. The Roman story I want to share, though, is about being repeatedly referred to as "he" and "him" during my first couple times in the store.

I don't know exactly how many trans women shop at the Roman store near me, but I'm fairly certain I can count them on one finger. All of their clothes are from Turkey and the women who work there represent several countries from that general corner of the world. Draw appropriate conclusions about overall familiarity with open gender non-conformity and respecting pronouns

and all that other challenging stuff associated with people like me.

The first time I overheard one of the ladies tell another "He wants to try these tops on" I convulsed in shame from behind the dressing room curtain where I was changing. I composed myself, stepped out, and didn't say a word as I paid for one of those tops that I just had to have.

During my next visit a few weeks later—I really, really love their clothes—one of the women referred to me as "he" as I was standing next to her. This time I said something, but I did it in a very gentle way. "Uh, actually, 'he' is not the right word to refer to me," and I pointed to the clearly feminine outfit that I was wearing. She apologized, I said it was ok, and I went back to trying on their clothes.

Then it happened again. Like, just a few minutes later. Ok, something needed to be done. I decided it was time for a spoonful of sugar, and I was going to deliver it in a most delightful way. *

I gathered the ladies in the store together—there were three of them working that day—and I explained to them with my sweetest smile and most benevolent eyes that if they ever fucking called me....

No, no, no that's not how it happened! Not at all! That energy does not run through me. I just thought it was a pretty good bit and wanted to make you laugh.

Anyway, I gathered the ladies together, gave them the five-minute version of my life story—I've always known but didn't know what to do about it, finally took the leap, really happy to be me, blah, blah, blah—and then turned around, pointed to my butt, and asked them: "Who has a nice butt?"

I made the hand gesture signaling that I expected an answer, and one of them sheepishly said "Uh....*she* does?"

"Correct!" I said. Then I asked the question again and had everyone say "She does!" at the same time.

Next question I asked: "Whose butt looks good in this skirt?" Wait for it...wait for it... "*Hers* does!"

We did this a few more times until everyone was smiling and laughing and that was the last time there were ever any issues.

I am very aware that in most circumstances there is a decent chance that I am one of the few, if not the first openly trans individual that the person I am interacting with has seen up close and in person. Where you live might be super progressive and all that and that's awesome, but in the grand scheme of things, the open participation of trans people in society alongside everyone else is still a rather fresh development.

In light of this, because I am openly and unmistakably trans, I am hyper aware that my every interaction with someone has a decent chance of informing their understanding of what the trans experience is.

I want to be clear that I am not speaking on behalf of the trans community, I am not a self-appointed ambassadress of transness, but I am one by default because that's just the way things are. I see this an opportunity to shape that person's perspective, not an obligation. For the most part I tend to seize that opportunity, but sometimes I do just want to sit there and get a manicure without having to tell my life story.

One other thing. I look at that photo of me in that gown and believe me, I understand why some people would hesitate to say "she" in response to my appearance. Just straight-up look at the photo and make a choice? Maybe it's a coin flip, I don't know. Throw in my voice, which back then was a little deeper than it is now, and I honestly get it, I really do.

The relevant point, though, is that I am more than my appearance, more than the outer shell. What I am finding so heartwarming, so genuinely meaningful to me as I go back and pull the content for this book together, is reflecting on how many people out there simply accepted me for me, regardless of how I looked.

It's a bit of an academic chicken-and-egg question: which came first, my Fuck You Confidence or people's acceptance of me? At this point, I'm not sure it matters outside of developing a six-step confidence-building workshop that I will make millions of dollars off of, but there is no question that the two are inextricably intertwined.

S1E10 | Cassandra Gets Emotional

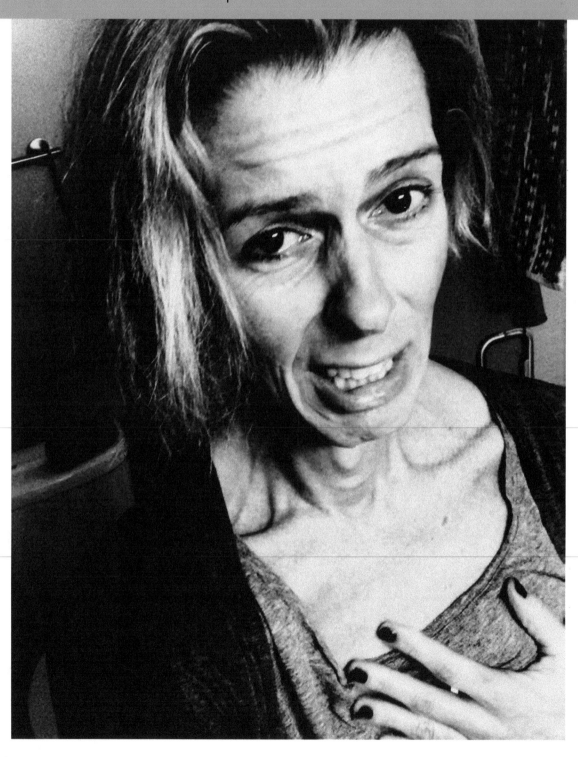

I've been doing a lot of thinking about this whole concept of Gender Euphoria lately and I think I'm starting to resent it. Look, I'm thrilled at my life and what my decision to transition has enabled. It's fantastic. But in spite of the curated narrative I present here, life is not a non-stop 24/7 adrenaline rush of unbridled joy. This might just be me, but I'm starting to chafe at feeling like that's the image I'm expected to present in order to 'justify' to society that I am something valid.

Any member of any marginalized group, when they finally are accepted into 'the club' feels some pressure to be on their best behavior, right? 'Wow, you let ME join YOUR club?!?! I'm so grateful, I PROMISE I won't let you regret this decision.'

You work harder. You smile more. You pay more attention to what you say. Whatever. You just got let into the Big Boys Club (usually literally) and you don't want to screw this up, not for yourself and not for any other member of your community. Because you know how the Big Boys think, right? One of us is acting up? Well then, we must all be bad apples.

Well, screw that. I want access to every single emotion a person can have, not just euphoria. Sometimes I might be sad, sometimes frustrated, sometimes—heaven forbid!—even angry. I want to be able to express these emotions without it triggering anything, without others thinking 'Well, so much for 'gender euphoria'—I guess it wasn't about the hormones after all.'

Far more importantly, I want to avoid the spiral of me thinking: 'Oh no, I'm sad today. I was sad before the transition. Maybe this isn't working? Maybe I'm always going to be sad! Maybe this was a huge mistake!!

Of course it wasn't a mistake! It's who I am and most of the time it's glorious.

And the story I share here reflects that and is 100% true. But it's not everything. And when it's not glorious, for reasons that have nothing to do with gender or hormones or whatever, just simply with day-to-day life, I want to be able to access those emotions without it calling into question my validity.

#gendereuphoria #thisshitishard
#thisisme

This was my first experience with the messy reality of life crashing headfirst into the curated "Everything is Awesome!" fantasy world of social media. I had kept the Smile Factory running non-stop for a couple months and this post represented my own need to keep things real, to make sure that I remained a person and did not turn into a persona. The "Mission, Vision, and Values" of my Instagram—a real range of emotions, heartfelt discussions of deep shit, and unretouched photos of me in my bra and panties—all started to come into focus here.

Getting to the point where sadness and disappointment, frustration and even anger have been reintroduced into my emotional range has been a long process that has involved a lot of work. Does the expression of these emotions look differently than before? Very much so. If it didn't, I would be concerned. But at the time I posted this, anything other than radiant joy was very triggering for me and caused me to wonder if all this effort was worth it.

Additionally, this is me starting to reckon with no longer being the societal mean, no longer having all that privilege I had earlier taken for granted. I was starting to appreciate through lived experience some small sliver of the challenges that so many others face, the vast majority of whom still contend with far more of an uphill climb than I ever have or ever will.

S1E11 | Cassandra Smiles Ironically

I remain astounded—maybe increasingly so—at the number of people from my 'previous life' who have outright rejected, abandoned, ignored, or 'forgotten' me for choosing transitioning over suicide.

The idea that in some way I was acceptable in their lives while I struggled and suffered to the point of wanting to end my life highlights for me how little I and my well-being really mattered.

The idea that literally almost nobody from those first 45 years wants anything to do with a person who chose to persevere, who is grounded and happy, and in some cases even thriving because of this decision blows my freaking mind.

Did you really need me to be miserable so you could feel ok about yourself? Is my happiness really that much of a threat to you? The fact that I wear a skirt? That I have breasts? Why did you need me to be who you needed me to be and not who I am?

My smile is genuine. You can't fake that. Waaaaaay too many pictures on my Insta. Way too much evidence. But goddamned, guys, that smile cost a lot.

I mean this: thank YOU for being part of this rebirth, for helping me push back against the doubts that still creep in about whether my happiness was worth all this loss, for letting me share my example and for sharing all of yours, from which I continue to learn so much.

#persevere #vulnerability

#vulnerabilityisstrength #phoenixrising

One of the narrative arcs that this book covers is my physical development. Hips, lips, and tits; that kind of stuff. Another storyline is the compression of several decades' worth of lost emotional growth—the whirlwind journey from rebirth through adolescence to grown-ass womanhood—into twelve very intense months. And yet another thread is my evolution as an artist.

I take Instagram very seriously as a creative sandbox, and over the past year I have gotten better at photography, styling, makeup, and marketing by playing in it. Learning the conventions of posting as a content creator has without a doubt made me a better writer, as well.

Alongside all of the above, I have also worked through a lot of emotional shit in plain view, anchoring the insights that I arrive at by showing my homework and putting them out there for others to see. This helps me set intentions, mark progress, and hold myself accountable so that I don't backslide.

Everything that I just mentioned is going on in this post.

S1E12 | Cassandra Enters Virgin Territory

Roses are red,
Violets are blue.
Guys in my DMs:
This post is for
you!

To the gentleman who wrote 'Roses are red, Violets are blue, If you fuck me, can I fuck you?' and to anyone who DMs me with a 'Hey...' or 'What's up?', I just wonder what's going on over there as you hit send. I'm serious!

Look, I'm not trying to chase anyone away and no names will be named, but can we talk?

I'm not gonna lie: that men find me a female worthy of hot pursuit is validating. Although I've come to learn that ANYTHING female, usually human, most often still with a pulse, is something that men will pursue, but still...

All of this is so brand new, at least to me. My life is like a woke AF reimagining of the Tom Hanks classic 'Big' just this time I'm a 13 year-old girl (hormonally) put into the body of a moderately hot middle-aged trans woman. I DONT KNOW WHATS GOING ON AND ITS ALL HAPPENING AT ONCE AND ITS OVERWHELMING! (side note: if anyone has any Hollywood connections, I know this is a solid idea—let's talk a script treatment and make this happen).

Like, for real: does 'Hey, wanna bang?' or 'Ur hot' really work? I want to know. What's the gameplan here? What's the calculus? Is it really this direct? This transactional?

I swear to you, I have zero idea what a male libido is given that my inner life has always been female. Back in high school when all my male friends would talk about 'getting some' I just wanted to talk about feelings. That's not every woman, but that was me. (side note: for anyone I was ever in a relationship with, this is why I listened to you talk about your mother. For hours.)

Gentlemen wherever you are—and it's a real We Are The World in my DMs— thanks for keeping it mostly classy. I will say this, though: never having experienced it up until a few months ago, the Male Gaze can be terrifying. And everything the Male Gaze can lead to, trans women experience it in a very concentrated form. So please: respect.

And if 'Hey, yur hot!' really works, you guys are getting off way too easy. Yes, that pun was fully intended.

#likeavirgin

#touchedfortheveryfirsttime

One of the things that I was really struggling with during this period was the huge gulf between the middle-aged female-presenting trans woman that people saw and the sexually naïve and emotionally immature teenager that I actually was. This post was my attempt—I think a rather successful one—to explain to others how much of a mindfuck this was.

Anyone who was attracted to me thought they were dealing with an adult, at least when it came to my body. I knew that was not the case, neither for my body, which was still rapidly evolving, nor for my emotional state. As you will see obliquely referenced in subsequent seasons, however, I ended up bridging this gap in a rapid and very intense way.

That said, the whole experience of moving from dating theory to dating practice is a storyline that I decided not to address in too much detail in this book. I did, however, spend a decent amount of time on Instagram sharing some of those experiences, so feel free to mine the archives if that interests you.

S1E13 | Ask Cassandra Anything

To my delight and surprise, my little baby Instagram has reached a milestone that I'm very humbled by: 1,000 Followers! In honor of that, let's do an "Ask Me Anything."

#1000followers #askmeanything

#isthisagoodidea

I did not set out to become an Influencer or a Fashionista or any specific thing when I started my Instagram. All I knew was that the Sephora video provided a compelling rationale for setting up an account and maybe an opportunity to do something with it. Aside from a bottomless well of self-absorption and a burning desire to connect with others, though, I didn't have a clue what I was doing.

By the time I posted this "Ask Me Anything," though, I understood that something was happening. I was beginning to express some fluency in Instagramese as my fifth language and becoming aware that my use of the platform as a "living diary of my transition" was itself transitioning, from a journal of what was happening to a means of expanding my horizons. I was also beginning to find my voice as a trans woman with something to say and starting to appreciate that others were interested in what I was saying.

Question: When did you start dressing in women's clothing?

Answer: I'll sum it up this way: I had a love/shame relationship with women's clothes for decades, going back to a very young age. Always the same thing: brief moments of feeling some kind of calm I simply couldn't explain and then TONS of shame as the only way I could process how wrong it was for me, a 'man' to be wearing these kinds of clothes. Thanks to the Internet and hearing the stories of so many people who went through similar cycles I got closer to figuring out what my deal actually was. And now I just dress. As myself. In clothes that finally come close to expressing the woman who has always been there.

Question: How did you develop your sense of style?

Answer: In the months before I started my social transition, I binge-watched about 20 seasons of Project Runway and it's spinoffs. Like, obsessively. I'd like to think a little bit of that sunk in. So many wonderful women have given me advice and feedback and just helped me find my groove, but the staff at my local Anthropologie stores have been particularly amazing. I feel like I've been adopted by them and they were the first fitting rooms where I felt comfortable stepping out and being seen by other women.

Question: What is your favorite part of being a woman so far? The makeup? The clothes?

Answer: My favorite part is just finally openly being who I've always been. After roughly 40 years of hiding and repressing and feeling shame at the incredible disconnect between who I am and who I felt like I had to pretend to be, just living openly as myself is infinitely amazing. Like, every freaking thing I can now just appreciate...as me! And yeah, I kind of like experimenting with my eye makeup game as well.

S1E14 | Cassandra Discovers Bags

MAMA GOT A BRAND NEW BAG!!

My favoritest person in the whole wide world came through with a #betterlatethannever Christmas gift that took my smile to 11. Like, Spinal Tapped the shit out of my normal daily allotment of joy.

The look, the feel, the heft, the balance, the proportions…I could go on and on about this effing bag. Total #loveatfirstsight #prythisfrommycolddeadhands action going on here.

Yes, I'm aware there is a geopolitical crisis on the verge of erupting in the Middle East over the targeted killing of the commander of the Quds Force. I get that. BUT THIS BAG!!!

#transpositivity #icandiehappynow #priorities #wheresmymodelingcontract

I cannot stress this enough: everything that I am presenting here happened in real time. All of it. The evolution in style, the emerging confidence, the growing command of an increasingly feminine body: what you see is what happened, as it happened.

As I look back at the posts from around this time, I am beginning to see the "me" that I currently am. I see that adolescent stage being left behind and the emergence of the woman who is writing these words. I see the first hints of what life is, not the promise of what it could be.

I also see the bags of recycling in the background. Pure coincidence, but really ties in well with the title of this episode, right? I only noticed them for the first time while reviewing photos on my much larger computer screen. Normally I look at photos on my phone, which is where I take them, review them, post them, and stare at them for hours.

Air Date: January 6, 2020

S1E15 | Cassandra Tends Barre

Without a doubt, one of the hardest, scariest things I've ever done was to walk into a Pure Barre studio last summer and inquire about taking classes. I would say that aside from the first time I went to see a physician about getting hormones it was probably the most nerve-wracking, most intimidating experience of my transition.

I had just legally changed my name, had just begun to rock an assortment of floral prints at work, and was starting to expect people to use the proper pronoun, but I knew that I needed to push myself further. I wanted to challenge myself to achieve something that had seemed impossible.

So I joined a cult.

From the moment I walked in and introduced myself as Cassandra Grace, I have worked my ass off (and more recently ON as I pay more attention to proper form during seat) to reshape my body and earn the respect and acceptance of the women around me through hard work. I haven't asked anyone for anything other than a spot in the back because I'm tall AF and I don't want to block the mirror for anyone else.

Soon I will have taken my one hundredth class. I can honestly say it will be one of the most significant achievements of my life, representing so much more than just a tight butt and lean legs.

Trans women are women, every kind of woman. There is no set narrative to what a 'trans woman' is, just like there is no set narrative to what a woman is. This trans woman is a #basicbitch femme suburban mom who joined a fitness cult, and I'm super proud to rep that day in and day out.

#priorities #icandiehappynow #wheresmymodelingcontract #transpositivity

First of all, I still haven't taken the recycling out. I merely arranged it neatly against the wall. THE RECYCLING ROOM IS LITERALLY RIGHT DOWN THE HALL! WTF?!

On a somewhat more serious note, I believe with every atom of my being that starting Barre just a few months after I went to a full dose of estrogen somehow supercharged my physical transition. I don't know exactly how, but I believe there is some kind of metabolic correlation between the specific kind of exercise that Barre represents and how my body has evolved. Also, "metabolic correlation" just sounds really smart, right?

There are multiple approaches to Male-to-Female HRT: some girls like me take pills, others get their estrogen through patches, and some really brave bitches give themselves injections. This is partly provider-dependent, partly personal preference. That said, the science is still evolving as far as which approach is more effective and why, especially as more and more of us get the life-saving care that we need and the longer-term impacts of various approaches can be looked at even more methodically.

What I am saying is that I just have this feeling that Barre has done more than give me confidence: I really think it helped to enhance the impact of the estrogen I have been taking. Study me, scientific community.

S1E16 | Cassandra Takes A Selfie

If you had told me a year ago that I would one day spend a rewarding afternoon sitting in public taking selfie after selfie without a care for what anyone around me was thinking, I would have laughed.

If you had told me the same thing but added that I'd be doing this as Cassandra Grace, successfully having navigated a full social transition.

If you had told me all of the above and included the detail about the Barbie blouse I would have told you to take your drugs and fuck right off because I only want the fun drugs, not the ones that do lasting harm.

And I would have felt really sad at the idea of my lifelong dream being mocked.

Bit by bit, step by step, I've come to a place that is so far beyond the wildest hopes and dreams I had about how this could actually turn out.

Take a step toward your dream. Then take another. And keep going. Whatever your dream, whether it's connected to your identity or your profession or your relationship or your body or whatever - that first step forward is really hard. The second is even harder. But if you make it to the third you have a good chance of going further than you ever thought possible.

#bethechange

This is kind of a nice feel-good moment of arrival, no? Buckle up. Things are about to go Next Level.

SEASON TWO

COUNTDOWN TO V-DAY

S2E1 | Cassandra Makes An Announcement

Last week a friend asked me 'So, uh, are you photoshopping your pictures or did you just get really good at tucking?'

First of all, anyone who knows anything about Barre knows that 'tucking' is an integral part of class, so yes, I'm really good at contracting my abs. Also, 'photoshopping' WTF?! That #thighgap action is 100% legit and something I'm very proud of given how hard I've worked to shape dem legs. Photoshop? Please...

That being said, in my friend's question I heard the Universe whispering to me: 'Girl, it's time to put this out there.' So with that, I'd like to share that in three months I'm getting some business taken care of downtown that is going to make the bikini pictures I intend to post over the summer SO much easier to take.

And yes, I intend to Instagram the heck out of the experience.

One of my favorite lines from Season One of Pose was when Angel was asked to show her genitals to the wife of the man she was sleeping with. Oh, sorry, uh, Spoiler Alert! Anyway, Angel's response to this says it all, at least for me: 'If you want to know anything about who I am, that's the last place you should look.'

Everyone has their own path. You do you. Let me do me. Period. As I talk about this, then, please know that I am only speaking for myself and only sharing my experience as one that may or may not resonate with anyone else's experience. But I believe it is important to share what I'm doing for the purposes of me being authentic.

So for me personally, I can't refer to this as 'Gender Confirmation Surgery.' My gender 'confirmation' took place last summer when my social transition began to take hold and I began to be treated by others as the woman I've always been. Hearing my name, having my pronoun used by strangers, walking out and about as me, that was all the gender confirmation I needed.

As I legally changed my name, as I got the 'F' on all my documents, as I began to hear 'ma'am' and 'her' and 'she' more and more often, nobody ever asked to look at my business. Because it wasn't theirs.

Once I began to exist in the world as me, though, my brain kept on telling me: 'Uh, girl, uh, that fuzzy splotch in the mirror that you just look past and ignore every time you get dressed? You know, that THING? Uh, just saying here, uh, maybe we can do something about that because I don't know what the hell that is and it's kind of annoying me.'

Fine.

So I scheduled my surgery four months ago and now that it's right around the corner I feel like it's time to share. Like everything I post, I never assume what someone's reaction will be and I am not doing that now.

I'm an open book kind of person, though, so if I'm going to share my experience with buying clothes, I just feel like I should be open about this as well.

#openbook #comingsoon #itstime

W<small>OW</small>.

Yes, that's my reaction to reading this now. Very insightful, I know, but the amount of foreshadowing going on here is off the charts. I should probably let you discover that for yourself. I don't want to spoil the plot twists. But OMG...

Since I mentioned Photoshop, though, I will mention how critical it has been for me to present unretouched photos, something that I discuss in more detail in a post appearing in Season Three. As I got more creative in taking photos, I learned to play with lighting and perspective and various other elements of composition. This photo represented a step forward in that regard, both artistically, and, uh...literally.

S2E2 | Cassandra Gets In The Game

There is a locally-owned upscale women's clothing store in my neighborhood that held a 'Single Ladies Night' tonight. Munchies, drinks, and the opportunity for a one-on-one interview with a matchmaking firm to see if you are a good fit for their clientele.

Challenge accepted.

To be totally honest—which is kind of my deal—I was spoiling for a fight. 'Tell me I don't belong! Tell me I'm not woman enough! Look at me sideways, I beg you!'

These were the thoughts in my head as I walked in the door. I was ready to throw down, to stand my ground as just as valid a woman as any other, to defend my right to be out and about as myself and who are you to say otherwise?

Instead, I had the most delightful time in the company of some wonderfully supportive women who were interested in my story and enthusiastic about my prospects. Period, full stop.

I don't know if anything will come of this other than one trans woman spent a couple of hours in the company of a lot of other women and that being the most normal thing in the world. And if that's all that comes of it, then at least for me, that's an evening well spent.

Also, this was the outfit I wore to the event. Slayed.

#slayallday #steppingout #debutante
#getinthegame #mommahasneeds

Every single step I've taken throughout the course of my transition has been hard AF. Every one. My joy and satisfaction (self-satisfaction?) at the steps I've taken are glaringly obvious, but every new one is hard. I may not have any shame, but I still confront fear every time I step into something new.

This was one of those moments. The big difference here, though, was that I was looking forward to the confrontation. I remember very clearly the "fighting spirit" I was feeling as I parked my car and walked over to the store for this event. I was truly hoping for something, anything, to trigger the passionate defense of my equal rights as a cougar like any other that I had practiced all afternoon long.

Just imagine my disappointment when I was welcomed with open arms and, by the end of the evening, had become the life of the party. Bummer.

While this marked a bit of a Turning Point in my approach to confronting fear, nothing has really changed when it comes to fear being an ever-present factor when I take some new step. I've come to welcome that feeling of apprehension as a harbinger of growth and that gives me the courage to step into it. I know that whatever lies on the other side is usually worth the effort.

S2E3 | Cassandra Has A Pretty Good Day

It was a pretty good day.

Absolutely crushed it at work while killing it in this outfit, a marriage made in heaven between my @spanx high waisted slacks and this beautifully draped-in-all-the-right-places blouse from @shopromanusa brought together in Holy Union by the leather belt I picked up from them as well.

And the shoes!! Finally wearing Big Girl shoes and could not be happier. I think they're in the second picture. Thoughts?

I also received the pre-op packet for my surgery. V-Day is now but ten weeks away and I am starting to truly freak out as I think about what's coming. Everyone I've talked to tells me I should expect to feel more confident in myself afterwards. Uh... excuse me?

#ootd #ootdfashion

#whatiworetowork #buymeadrink

While this is a fairly straightforward "Dear Diary: today was good" type of post, it is also a solid example of the kind of content that you find all over Fashion Instagram. The only thing missing is a seemingly randomly generated inspirational quote. I cannot tell you how many times I have seen a Parisian breakfast spread paired with "something-something follow your dreams."

I wasn't trying to replicate that here, but the subliminal influence of being inundated with those kinds of posts is pretty evident. I do think the outfit description is pretty tight, though, and an obvious expression of my growing fluency in fashion.

Also, look at that pre-COVID innocence on display! Ten weeks to go before the thing I have been waiting for my entire life finally happens! What could possibly go wrong?

S2E4 | Cassandra Serves Some Looks

I've gotten a lot of comments recently about how comfortable I look in front of the camera. Someone with an excellent eye even said that I 'wear it like a crown.' It got me thinking 'why?' and I think I have a pretty solid answer.

Back in The Miserable Years I craved validation. Thirsted for it. Every teacher or professor or boss was a surrogate parent whose approval would give me meaning. Everything I did for the people close to me, I needed to be told how great it was, i.e., how great I was. The validation of others gave me purpose and filled the void at the center of my identity.

But it didn't. That void was infinite and the more I tried to fill it with validation, the more frustrated and disappointed and disillusioned I became about ever feeling like a complete person.

Once I began to transition, though, the void began to disappear. Now it's gone. And in its place is a radiantly confident sense of self I have never, ever experienced. And instead of seeking validation, now I want attention. And I want it because I'm proud of who I am, proud of what I'm doing, and shamelessly (literally without shame) putting myself out there.

But I'm doing it from a position of confidence. There is no 'am I good? Please tell me I'm good!' Instead these pictures represent me saying 'I'm good. Enjoy.'

The difference between needing validation and wanting attention, at least for me, is the difference between asking others to define me and knowing with full confidence who I am.

#transpositivity #bethechange
#whatiworetoday #selflove
#selflovejourney

A lot of my posts—this one for example—reflect a "summing up" of work that I do in therapy. I'll unpack some particular dysfunction or aspect of my trauma and then anchor my progress in understanding it by putting it out there for others to tell me what a great outfit I am wearing or how hot my ass looks.

That's just how Instagram works. All this serious stuff I post is swimming against the stream. There are, however, a surprising number of people who find the serious stuff compelling, and it is a delight to connect with them and engage in rich and meaningful conversations. Some of those conversations are so rich and so meaningful, though, that every once in a while, I do enjoy just posting a throwaway bra and panty pic and calling it a day.

I wrote this ahead of Valentine's Day while in the beginning stages of the healthiest relationship I have ever had: the one with myself. Looking back, it's a good thing that finally happened given how much alone time I was about to have.

S2E5 | Cassandra Is Invited To Show Off Her Butt

So I get an email the other day inviting me to a 'special event' for Lululemon, part of their launch of a new material for their leggings, Everlux.

I know what you're thinking: 'CASSANDRA, YOU ARE NOT AN INFLUENCER!!' Believe me, that's what I was thinking too as I wondered why the hell I got this email. But wait, it gets better.

Not only was I invited to this event—it takes place later this month—but I was also invited to come into my local store and try on leggings with this new material. And not just 'try on' but actually receive a pair free of charge so I could wear them for this event.

What the what?!?!

So that's what you see in these pics here— me trying on different leggings and having the absolute time of my life AS PEOPLE DISCUSS WHICH ONES MAKE MY BUTT LOOK BETTER! There is no better feeling than to have several women stand next to me and have an educated, serious conversation about which leggings my butt looks better in. (Narrator: her butt looks good in all of them)

I ended up choosing a badass black camo print and while the Special Event isn't for another few weeks, I can't wait to go to Barre class and try my new leggings out in real-world conditions.

I can't even begin to convey how honored I am to have been invited to participate in this. I don't feel comfortable speaking for anyone but myself, but I know that everywhere I go and everything I do, people look at me and think 'trans.' I'm REALLY proud of that and want to do my best so that whatever association anyone makes with that word is a positive one.

#lululemon #lululemonambassador

#thatbutttho #pinchmeimdreaming

I remember stepping into this store for the first time back in September of 2019, shortly before I got on Instagram and started producing the epic content you are now thoroughly enjoying. By then I had been taking Barre classes for a few months and I decided to reward my commitment by splurging on the ultimate status symbol for my butt: a pair of Lululemon leggings.

Here I am five months later, at the invitation of Lululemon, trying on a complimentary pair of leggings that I would receive in exchange for posting some content on Instagram. I was chosen as one of several local "Sweat Influencers"—women with notable social media presences in the fitness realm—to help promote the debut of this new material.

When it comes to the brand names that you see in this book, there is a method to my materialistic madness. I remember what it was like to shamefully throw a clearance-priced bottle of foundation into my shopping cart and hope against hope that nobody noticed. I remember what it was like lifting weights in the gym, trying so hard to bulk up but secretly dreaming of having the lithe physique of a ballerina. I remember hiding the disgust I felt for my body under bulky and formless clothes.

When I decided to commit to my transition in early 2019, I set my aim as high as I possibly could as far as the spaces that I wanted to earn my place in. All those stores where guys stand outside looking at their phones? Feeling at home in those places was an incredibly important metric of success for my transition. Yes please, I would like a sample of that serum. What do you ladies think of this top? Does my butt look better in the Align or the Wunder Under?

The status I was seeking wasn't explicitly the brand, but what the brand represented to me: the highest bar of social acceptance as a woman that I could imagine. The look on my face in these photos is the look of someone who has achieved more than she ever dreamed possible. And was already dreaming of more.

S2E6 | Cassandra Goes on an Anthropological Excursion

One year ago I walked into an Anthropologie store a sweaty, nervous mess, utterly terrified at what I was about to do: try on clothes. I was hiding in plain sight under a very androgynous presentation. I wasn't yet on a full dose of Hormone Replacement Therapy, hadn't come out at work, hadn't done anything but make the decision that it was time to do something.

One year later and I got a tour of their Corporate Headquarters in Philadelphia at the invitation of one of my guardian angels, the generous and wonderful @jayel_mcguinn. It was thanks to her that I walked in that fashion show last September, an event that has truly changed the course of my life.

There have been so many milestones and turning points over this past year, but as I start to plot my Next Steps in life, I point to that experience as one that was pivotal.

It wasn't just the Anthro team that took care of me. Dozens of people got to see a tall, lanky trans woman—me—proudly represent the clothes that help express herself to the world. The other women who walked with me welcomed me into their sorority with open arms and continue to support my baby Insta as she grows up.

I am so grateful to all of these wonderfully generous women for their effort to help make possible days like today, like yesterday, and honestly like every single day of this reincarnated life I am lucky enough to lead.

#gratefulthankfulblessed #pinchme #transvisibility #anthrogirl

Like, what is going on here? What kind of Make-A-Wish insanity was I living? The change in my life over the previous twelve months—from sheepishly entering a store I thought I had no business in to being given a VIP tour of their corporate headquarters—I mean, WTF?!

I remember this period as one of manic intensity in the run-up to bottom surgery. I wanted to put as many balls in motion as I could before a few were removed for good. Oh come on! How can I not make that joke?

But for real, I was trying to lay the groundwork for some kind of presence in the fashion world post-surgery. I had vague dreams of being Anthropologie's first middle-aged trans model, someone who would carry the banner of age and gender positivity. Ok, that wasn't a vague dream. That was a very specific dream, one of several I had related to setting the bar for myself even higher than the one I was currently vaulting over.

I wanted to prove that I belonged, that all these experiences weren't just the result of people humoring me or throwing some charity my way. That I earned my spot under the sun.

Representation matters and I was starting to think that maybe I could represent something to others. I was connecting the dots from all these experiences and beginning to feel that I not only belonged, but that I had something to say.

To be clear, the limit of my ambition at this time was modeling. I wanted my very transgender body walking another runway, my very transgender face in a campaign, on some magazine cover. I wanted to be the kind of representation that I never saw growing up.

S2E7 | Cassandra Goes on a Three-Hour Tour

Dear Hollywood: I would very much like to remake every TV and Motion Picture property with trans characters and suggest that we start with Gilligan's Island. I believe the role of Ginger should be mine. Thank you.

Let the bidding war between @netflix @ hbo @hulu @amazonprimevideo @disneyplus and @starz begin.

#wheresmymodelingcontract

#fashionista #gilligansisland #ginger

#threehourtour #remake

You may recall this gown from S1E2, my little homage to sartorial emancipation. I'm including it here for a couple of reasons.

One, I look amazing. I mean, that's a solid-enough reason. It's not just that I look amazing, though. I look...different. Same gown, totally different vibe. I'm not the kid in a candy store anymore, not the little girl just happy to be let into the Big Girl space. Hello, curves. Hello, bedroom eyes. Hello, uh, bedroom.

We are entering a period with these posts where I am starting to step into my femininity, starting to feel really, really comfortable in my own skin. Starting to feel comfortable enough to want someone else to feel my skin. You see where I'm going with this.

This was also the first post that kind of blew up, generating about twice as many "likes" as any of my previous high-performing posts. I'm going to do my best to spare you a diatribe about the Instagram Algorithm, but this post got such a reaction that I started to pay a lot more attention to metrics. Sadly, I know myself well enough that having just written that, at some point I will subject you to a diatribe about the Instagram Algorithm.

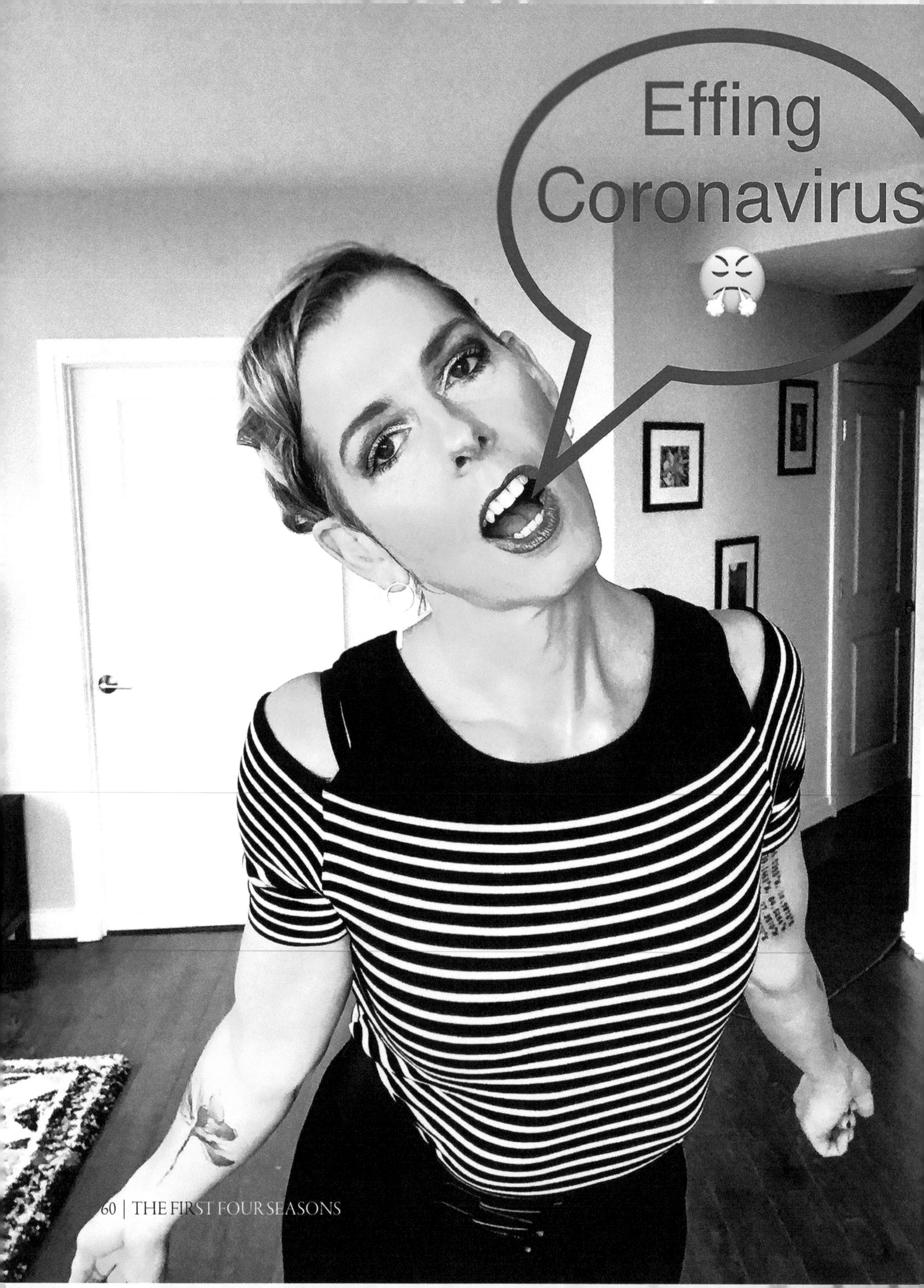
Effing
Coronavirus

S2E8 | Cassandra Gets Some Bad News

So a few days ago I enthusiastically—and in retrospect, stupidly—teased some 'exciting news' that I was awaiting confirmation of. Well, yesterday I got confirmation that it was happening and I was all excited to do a post about it...

And today I got confirmation that it is NOT happening because, well, coronavirus.

Crap.

The exciting news was that I was going to walk in the Spring Fashion Show that Anthropologie was holding in Bethesda in two weeks. Walking in the Fall Fashion Show last September was a grand coming out for me as far as my acceptance and inclusion by others and my own sense of confidence in myself.

I was really honored to have another such opportunity and was looking forward to comparing the experiences as a LOT has changed as far as my body and my sense of ownership over it since last September.

Sadly, because of coronavirus all the Anthro Spring shows have been cancelled. I don't know if that means people will no longer be shopping in stores or gathering in public places or even breathing in two weeks. I do know that I'm six weeks out from V-day, and if this freaking illness and the mass panic surrounding it gets in the way of my vajayjay, I'm going to be really pissed.

#coronavirus #bummer
#mime #modelforhire
#dontcountyourchickensbeforetheyhatch

Hₒw quaint.

S2E9 | Cassandra Gets Invited to the Kennedy Center

Yesterday was International Women's Day and for me personally it was also my One-Year Tranniversary of coming out and going to a full dose of HRT. A year ago I was not on Instagram, had not changed my name nor any of my documents, and was still presenting very androgynous.

One year later and I celebrated International Women's Day at the Kennedy Center in DC as a guest of Lululemon. The wonderful women organizing this celebration of women's resilience reached out and invited me because I am one of them: a resilient AF woman.

I post things here for several reasons. One, I feel that for the first time in my life I have things to share from a place of confidence and not from a place of insecurity. In other words, I welcome the attention but I don't crave the validation.

I share because I believe there is power in the everyday advocacy of loudly and proudly living my life as a trans woman in a world where being a woman is hard enough. But holy shit is it amazing and worth every effort. If someone can draw inspiration from my effort then I am paying forward the debt of inspiration I have from those who went before me.

I also post because I need a reminder that this is real. That after 47 years of existing in spite of myself, I need as many reminders as possible that this is not a dream now that I'm living AS myself, that I am not a prisoner to the past, that I am literally transcending.

I know that in a few weeks I will need a reminder that I marked my One-Year Tranniversary at the Kennedy Center with several hundred other women and that I left that event knowing that I belong, that I'm enough, and that this is indeed the life I deserve.

#iwd2020 #thesweatlife
#transvisibility #payitforward

I believe in the Universe. I believe in karma. I believe there is meaning in everything if we want to see it.

I came out to strangers on March 8, 2019. International Women's Day. I had not been planning to come out that day, but something compelled me to put on the floral pants that I first eyed during my inaugural trip to Anthropologie a month earlier. I wore those pants to work, got up in front of a group of strangers, and said the words: "Happy International Women's Day to all of you ladies. And to me as well."

I left that gathering and wrote a spontaneous email to everyone that I worked with telling them that I was transgender. I told them that I was still figuring out what was to come, but that they should expect a follow-up email with specific instructions on how they should treat me.

To be at the Kennedy Center one year later...to be there as a guest of Lululemon...to walk up to a mirror, turn around, point at my butt and have THESE messages in the background...this is all the proof I need that there is a Master Plan.

Yes, I am living my truth. Yes, I am empowering others to step into an extraordinary life. Yes, I am inspiring people to be....something, something, something. I can't really make the rest of it out, but I'm sure it's inspiring.

But honestly, when I took this picture all I was doing was pointing at my butt. The Universe sure does work in mysterious ways.

S2E10

Cassandra Confronts the Coming Coronapocalypse

It's the #coronapocalypse but make it fashion.

Here's the rest of my #ootd from yesterday. One thing that is blowing my mind as it gets warmer is that I'm starting to wear clothes that I bought last year Spring/Summer and the fit is SO different. Like, these curves were not here last year. Nor was the #sideboob

For those who appreciate it: you're welcome.

Hope everyone is finding whatever coping mechanism works for them and is going the extra mile to be kind to others.

#curves #legallyblonde #celebratelife

#legsfordays #fucoronavirus

While I did not mention this on my Instagram at the time, a few days prior to this post I had a consultation with my surgeon for Breast Augmentation. My bottom surgery was scheduled for 22 April and I was considering getting both procedures done at once. I hadn't yet made a decision, but the option was available to me and I was leaning in that direction.

Throughout the winter I did everything possible to increase the size of my breasts. I ate so much cheese, pounded pint after pint of Ben and Jerry's (Cherry Garcia was my boob food of choice), and drank crazy amounts of soy milk for the supposed boost of phytoestrogen that would make my little boobies swell with pride.

As every girl knows, though, boobs are fat and it's the first fat to go and the last to be added. I was exercising like a maniac, so no matter what I did, I never got more than a very, VERY modest B cup. And that's being generous.

I also remember this as one of the last times I went into the office. I am a resilient woman and I have made many a pitcher of lemonade since this was taken, but this is the hardest photo to look at of all the ones I have included in this book.

Full disclosure: I have been sobbing uncontrollably as I type these words. Going to keep this in here to "capture the moment" and all that, but I'm having a hard time seeing the screen right now.

This is the last photo I have from the Before Times, the last photo in which I recognize the hopeful innocence of the dream that I still believed possible. Clearly I have other dreams now. Clearly I am making them happen. Yay perseverance and all that.

Looking at this picture right this moment, though, I'm only just now appreciating what I lost.

Sorry guys...I need a minute. This photo is wrecking me.

S2E11 | Cassandra Is All Dressed Up With Nowhere to Go

As promised, here is a whole heaping serving of looks from last night's #coping shoot. There be videos as well.

As I mentioned to a number of you in the comments from that last post, I got this hot #lbd last fall and this was the first time I've actually worn it. Figured the End of the World was an appropriate occasion.

#legsfordays #datenightoutfit #fem-mefatale #werking #lewks

Every once in a while I will take a photo and my little brain just doesn't know how to process it. Like, there is no freaking way that I actually look like this. Whatever combination of lighting and angles and pixel dust combined to make these photos, I refuse to accept that this is in any way an accurate reflection of what I look like.

Praise on Instagram tends to be a mile wide and an emoji deep, so I tend not to put too much stock into compliments people give me on my appearance. I know they are well-intentioned and I both welcome and acknowledge them, but I have never let them play an important role in defining my self-image.

That said, because of dysphoria, because of how rapidly my sense of self was evolving, because of so many factors clouding an "objective" take on how I saw myself, I would often turn to the only person whose opinion I trusted on this issue: my therapist. Again and again I would pull up a photo that I had posted on my phone, show it to my poor therapist, and ask her if I really looked like that. Again and again she would sigh a little and say, "Yes."

In spite of everything that has changed, all that I have experienced since taking these pics, they still hold that kind of power over me. I look at them and say to myself, "No effing way..."

This post also marks the descent into madness associated with the uncertainty around whether my surgery would take place because of the COVID-related hospitalization surge. Fun times ahead.

S2E12 | Cassandra Lights Up The Dark

To everyone who is posting, whatever you are posting, please accept my thanks for your efforts. The content you create has become a huge source of support and comfort for me and I feel blessed to have met so many wonderful people on this platform.

To anyone who finds some kind of value in what I post, please accept my thanks for the appreciation that you show. Except for the dick pics. I really don't need any more of those. We're good, ok. Enough.

To anyone who is reading or has read something that I've written, please accept my thanks for letting my words find a home, however temporary, in your heart.

These are Dark Times for many and they are about to get darker for so many more. I'm not going to lie: I'm terrified at what the next several weeks could bring. I hope during this time I can put some measure of positive energy out into the world as gratitude for being able to bask in the energy that so many of you have shared with me.

Also, how about this dress, eh?
#goingoutinstyle

#vamp #transwoman
#lightinthedarkness #fuckcorona

I like juxtaposition. I like extremes. Showing both ends of a spectrum and playing in the space in between. My Instagram started off as a very literal "living diary" of my transition and rather quickly evolved into a sandbox for the performance art of my life.

I was sixteen, living in Hamburg, Germany, and during an overnight slumber party my then-best friend called me a "Lebenskünstlerin." I have retroactively corrected the gender of the German word that means "artist of life."

I am who I have always been. Transitioning hasn't made me a different person. Instead, it has freed me from the corrosive burden of trying to conform to a gender identity that does not align with who I am. My energy, my personality, my drive, my creative spirit, my thirst for knowledge and experience: all that is who I am. Being able to express all those things with my mind and body finally in sync, running on estrogen, represents a freedom of being that I am only now stepping into.

But the person I am is the person I have always been. Transitioning for me is about liberation from trauma. The trauma of a spirit trapped in a body that it does not recognize as its own.

S2E13 | Cassandra Gets Comfy on the Casting Couch

DEAR HOLLYWOOD: MAY I HAVE YOUR ATTENTION?

I'm concerned we might run out of shows to stream during this quarantine. I'm also concerned I will have nothing to do. I have solved both problems. Here are several ideas for shows. We can't do them all, but let's aim high.

SAVING GRACE: Could go in two directions: 1) A reboot of Touched By An Angel where I travel the world and heal people's emotional and spiritual wounds or 2) One of those shows like Breaking Bad where the main character is a monster and the dramatic tension over the arc of the series is whether or not she can be saved.

Bonus Idea: it starts off as the first one and then by the Season Three cliffhanger it turns into the second idea! In this case, we'll call the show FALL FROM GRACE. Oh, that's fucking genius!

AMAZING GRACE: This is the Marvel Universe show on Disney Plus where I'm a fashion model by day, superhero by night. Or is it the other way around? Either way: superpowers change with my hairstyle.

COUP DE GRACE: This one is a little higher-concept because we need people to focus on the spelling and not the pronunciation, but basically this is a series set in a dystopian future (April??) where I lead a revolution to overthrow the government.

STATE OF GRACE: This is the spin-off series that picks up 100 years later (think how they ruined Star Trek) and focuses on life in the fashion utopia that the events covered in the final season of COUP DE GRACE brought about.

#quarantineandchill #quarantinelife
#netflixandchill #agentneeded #coping

I dip my toes into lots of different communities on Instagram. I remember seeing post after post among the Wellness Guru/Yoga Maven/Life Coach crowd around this time, right when the pandemic was taking root, saying things like: "Listen to Mother Earth, She is sending us a message" or "How will YOU use this opportunity?" I remember thinking to myself, "Bitch, people are DYING!!! This is NOT a global wellness retreat!"

My indignation came from what I felt was clumsy and callous expressions of unacknowledged privilege. Like, people were risking their lives to make sure your fresh-pressed beet juice was still available, the least you could maybe do was not talk about how you were going to use this "pause" to perfect your Downward Dog.

And yet, in what ways am I any different? Maybe my messages of perseverance and my expressions of cathartic creativity come across a little differently, but that's just my personality, my quirks. The fundamental intent of what I am doing, though, isn't really all that different than what was in those messages, however tone deaf I thought they were.

I remember reacting very strongly to those posts—FFS white girls, check your privilege!!!—but not saying anything. I wasn't sure how to communicate what I was feeling in a constructive way. As a guiding principle, I'm not online to shout others down, to "cancel" them, or to call them out.

A little bit down the road, though, I found the voice I was looking for and I started to use it.

S2E14 | Cassandra Calls Out Corporate America

Good Morning, Corporate World! I have a message for YOU on this Trans Day of Visibility.

We need you. That's the message. We need you to raise our visibility every day, not just today. Seeing us represented alongside others sends a powerful message to EVERYONE: to those like me who desperately want to see ourselves portrayed as equal to everyone else and to everyone else who will increasingly see us as equal to them.

We need you more than ever because in so many cases our governments are dropping the ball, if not outright kicking us in them. If we still have them. It's a figure of speech. Moving on...

Some of you are doing a good job and I've even had the pleasure of partnering with companies like Anthropologie, Sephora, Roman USA, and Lulu Lemon.

Thank you for those opportunities. They made a difference to me and others who saw them. Let's see more, on a more regular basis, with a much broader representation of the trans experience.

We buy your products. Or maybe some of us want to buy your products but don't feel welcome to do so. As a trans woman, some of the most utterly terrifying moments OF MY LIFE were those first times I started to shop for myself. As myself. Make it easier for us.

Please.

#transproud #transpride

I consider my life to be my advocacy, and living it in an open, proud, and highly visible way is my form of influence.

What am I an advocate for? Well, as this post makes pretty clear, I consider myself to be an advocate for the trans community, even if I am not necessarily a member of that community. More on that next season.

I am also an advocate for corporate responsibility. For the transformative power of evolutionary change. I am an advocate for the healing power of kindness, for the grace of the Holy Trinity of Tolerance, Acceptance, and Inclusion. I am an advocate for equity and equality.

This is not some ex post facto grafting of legitimizing purpose onto the gift of free athleisure wear. I lucked into a tiny platform in response to my letter of gratitude to Sephora. Ever since that moment, I have been relentlessly intentional in building that platform out to reach more and more people.

In response to this post, the lovely people at Laura Mercier invited me to rep their fine product.

S2E15 | Cassandra Smiles For The Camera

To everyone who tells me to smile more: thank you SO MUCH for that suggestion! You have no idea how validating that feels! Nothing, absolutely NOTHING makes me feel more like a woman than being told to smile more. Thank you for being such a special part of my journey!

To everyone else who respectfully admires my pictures or thoughtfully appreciates what I write—or both!!—please accept a very sincere thank you for being part of something that is very meaningful to me. Maybe more than you know.

As I find myself struggling to get through each day—and sometimes wondering if I even should—having this outlet has literally been a saving grace. I know, I know. But it's true. As the world is in crisis, I am dealing with my own personal apocalypse and that is no exaggeration. Details forthcoming.

My relationship with the camera sometimes feels like the healthiest one I've ever had, and the exhibitionist in me enjoys putting our torrid romance on display for you to enjoy. Some of you enjoy it a LOT. You're welcome. I enjoy that you enjoy it. Thank you.

'Надежда умирает последней' is a Russian saying that has always been a mantra for me: 'Hope is the last thing to die.' I am clutching at whatever hope I can to make it to that next day. And the one beyond.

In the meantime, I know the dipshits who tell me to smile more haven't read a word of this. And God help anyone who leaves a comment along the lines of 'that's more like it!'

To everyone else: I've only ever wanted to keep this real, and if you ask me how I've been, you should know I won't play pretend.

#persevere #smilemore #coping

#quarantinelife #nofilter

First of all, the number of women who did not read this caption but reflexively left a comment along the lines of "Great smile!" or "So beautiful, you should smile more!" blew my mind. Really, ladies?

But I wasn't all that surprised. I knew that those were responses from women who hadn't read what I wrote because they were furiously working to please our insatiable overlord, the Instagram Algorithm. Allow me to explain...

If you are using Instagram to post a cute video of the sandwich your son fed your dog so that Aunt Betsy in Oklahoma can see it, then you don't need to care about The Algorithm. All you need to care about is that Aunt Betsy sees the video and leaves a comment telling you how cute your son is. If she doesn't, she's dead to you. That's how Instagram works for a lot of people.

If, however, you are an aspiring Influencer who dreams of offering your Followers a personalized 20% discount,

perhaps on their first purchase of the hair oil infused with baby seal tears that changed your life, then you need to care about The Algorithm. A lot.

Instagram doesn't care how many Followers you have. Instagram doesn't care how compelling—or not—your content is. All Instagram cares about is that you engage with other accounts to create the data that Instagram then sells to its clients. If you do that, if you "engage" and thereby create product for Instagram to sell, then The Algorithm will confer blessings on your content and raise its visibility among your Followers.

Oh yes, that's right. Even for those with tremendous numbers of Followers, if you—or in the case of Very Famous People, your interns—don't make the bare minimum effort to "engage" on others' Instas, then your Followers may not see your content when it is posted. It is more likely to get bumped down someone's Feed (the stream of content you see from the people you follow) and drowned out by other posts from those who are engaging more.

But wait, there's more! In order to secure Influencer deals with companies, you have to demonstrate a certain level of engagement by others on your own Instagram. In other words, companies want to see a certain percentage of your Followers actively engaging with your content—usually around 2-3% of your total Follower base—before they will view your platform as a viable partner.

Let's say your husband bought you 100,000 Followers as a Birthday Gift. Yay, you're an Influencer! No, no you aren't. Just try posting that photo of yourself feeding swans in an evening gown and see what happens when you get a few hundred "likes" and fifteen comments. We all know what's going on. And so do companies, none of which is going to give you that sweet, sweet MELANIA20 code that you were counting on.

You have to hustle, and you have to hustle non-stop. So among those trying to get Influencer gigs, there is an unspoken "like for like" agreement that turns much of fashion and beauty Instagram into an endless cacophony of "Obsessed!" and "Too cute!" and "Stunning!"

Over and over and over again, on every single fucking post.

As soon as I realized this, my love relationship with Instagram turned into a love-hate relationship. It's one thing to hear about the ways in which social media algorithms manipulate users, another thing to actively feel and be conscious of the manipulation as it is taking place. The Greater Good of building out my platform to help support my Bigger Picture goals has always won out, but Holy Fuck have there been moments when I've wanted to step away in disgust at my awareness of being an indentured servant in Mark Zuckerberg's digital salt mine.

I told you that rant was coming.

As far as the references to "personal apocalypse" and struggling to make it through the day in this post, by this point I was convinced that my surgery was not going to happen. The hospital had been cancelling elective surgeries in two-week blocks and it was just a little over two weeks until my date. I had been contacting my surgeon's office every couple of days, tearfully begging for clarity about whether my surgery would take place. Every time I got the same answer: your surgery is still scheduled, as of now it's on.

But I saw what was happening in the world, saw where things were trending. I saw these two-week windows of cancelled procedures getting closer and closer to my date and it seemed inevitable that mine would be cancelled as well. I was a total mess, shaking throughout the day with anxiety and uncertainty, utterly terrified about what would happen if my vagina slipped through my fingers.

You know what I mean.

And yet there was hope. In fact, the day after I posted this, the hospital called me and conducted my pre-op interview. As soon as I got off the phone, I popped the first pill my primary care physician had prescribed to help me manage the hormonal disruption of going off estrogen ahead of surgery. Hope had not yet died.

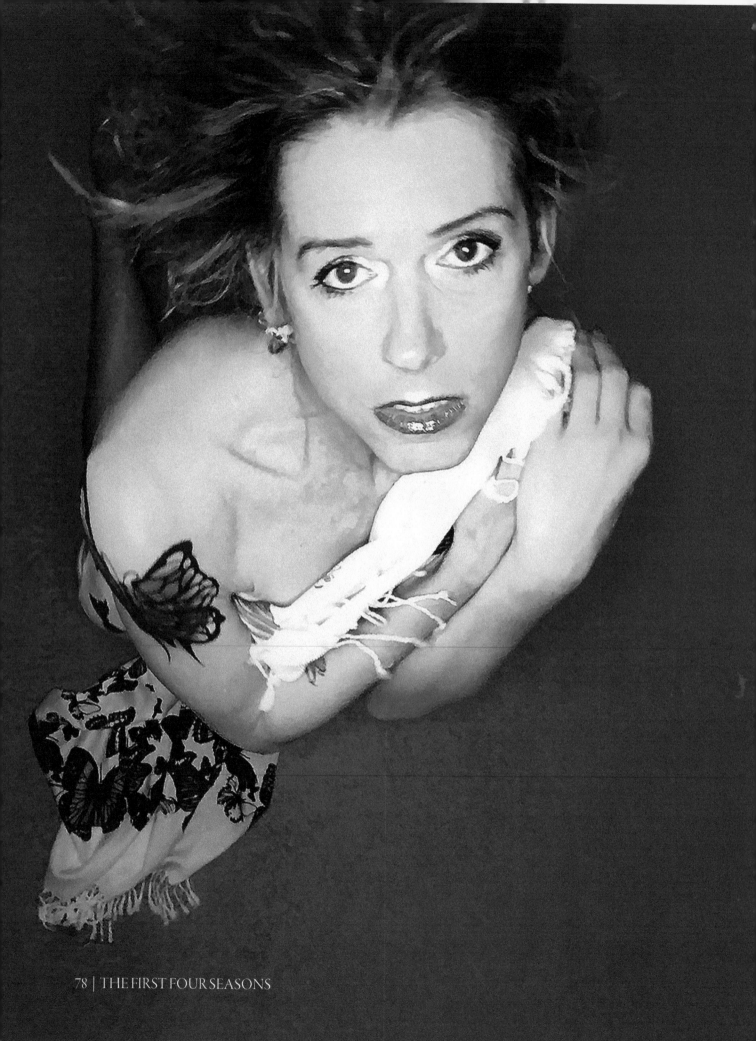

S2E16 | Cassandra's Vagina Slips Through Her Fingers

I've prided myself on keeping it real here and it's meant a lot to me to do so. So in that spirit, this is as real as it gets.

I found out this morning that my bottom surgery has been cancelled. I was two weeks away. The earliest it can be rescheduled is 26 January of next year.

As the world is on pause, my world feels like it's ending. Not because I placed concrete hopes and dreams on my vagina, but because this was 'simply' the culmination of all my efforts, the through-the-looking-glass moment when everything would come together into a unified whole. I had no plan for what it would look like, but I had a plan that involved it actually happening.

Surgery represented no more repressing, no more overcompensation, no more willing myself to push past the inadequacy and incompleteness of my body. Instead, it offered the promise that I could finally transcend those limitations and just be.

My gender is not being denied by this not happening, but it's also not being affirmed in the way I and I alone need it to be. This was to be my moment, the beginning of the rest of my life, also the beginning of a new life. All of that at once.

I understand that millions of people have lost something as a result of this plague. A wedding. A vacation. A life. I get that. But this is my loss and right now it is all-encompassing.

So I don't know what this means. I'm going to stick around and respond to any comments that roll in because I do treasure this community, then I need to step away and decide if I want to keep going.

To anyone who drew inspiration from anything I posted over these past six months, I hope this doesn't invalidate whatever you gained from what I shared. I also want to thank everyone who has inspired and supported me.

Many ends turn out to be new beginnings. Maybe that's the case here and maybe it isn't. Right now I just don't know. That's what's so hard—because I always knew.

#heartbreak #vulnerability #fuckcorona

T o be continued...

SEASON THREE

QUARANTINE QRAZY

S3E1 | Nevertheless, Cassandra Persisted

I'm back. Was tempted to wait until Sunday, but that would have been just a little too on the nose, even for me.

Having my surgery postponed at THIS moment in my life—for reasons that are very personal and I have not shared here—felt like the hardest thing I've ever had to overcome, and I've been around the block.

My mother abandoned me as a child. I ran away from an abusive home at 15. I put myself through college. Had my first child at 22. Learned three languages and studied two more. Was married to a Russian. Twice. Lost my soulmate.

This experience has been the hardest to manage.

Being able to grieve with everyone here is very meaningful. Thank you for all the love and support. Even the guy who DM'd me 'nice ass.' What can I say? He's not wrong.

I made the decision to get surgery roughly eight months ago. My vagina didn't make it to term. My new surgery date is a little over nine months from now. As a trans woman, it's the closest I'll ever get to giving birth, so I'm going to embrace the hell out of that. I expect a shower.

Literally everyone on this planet has been affected by this crisis. If this ends up being how it affected me, then I will consider it a blessing. Yeah, I got knocked down, but I'm not even close to staying there.

#thistooshallpass #igotthis
#neverthelessshepersisted
#resilience #transisbeautiful

"Many ends turn out to be new beginnings..."

That was the hopeful "ray of light" that I was clinging to when I announced that my surgery had been cancelled and then proceeded to stage a funeral for my unborn vagina on Instagram. Among many other things that this stage of my evolution represented, the shift from "Hi, I'm just so happy you let me join this party!!!" to "Bitch, give me the mic, this diva has a few things to say" was complete.

For the record, it's pronounced Ca-SAHN-dra. Rhymes with DRAH-ma.

As I work on this book, I also continue to post on Instagram. In fact, having fully embraced the convention of episodic content covering narrative arcs, I just wrapped up Season Five and am taking a minor hiatus to push the book as close as I can to the finish line before kicking off Season Six.

I mention that because toward the end of 2020 I posted something about my rescheduled bottom surgery. I am including it here in full as it best reflects where my head is currently at in relation to what you just read. The following post is from 24 November 2020, in case you want to check out the incredible photo that I reference:

Since many Americans decided that being a selfish dumbass was more important than my vagina, I'm fairly confident that my surgery will be cancelled again. It is scheduled for late January, but with hospitalizations surging right now, things don't look good. Perhaps if the CDC had run a public awareness campaign along the lines of "Think of Cassandra's vagina: wear a mask" we wouldn't be in the mess we are in.

On second thought, I'm not sure if I want my hoohah to be associated with mask-wearing. Actually, I'm pretty sure I don't.

How about this one: "Cassandra's Vagina: Stop the Spread." Nope. That's a nope.

Regardless, the virus is out of control here and it seems obvious to me that the butterfly I have been chasing for nearly fifty years is again going to flutter out of reach.

The last time this happened back in April, I went into a cave for three days and re-emerged with ridiculous amounts of creative energy. I ▓▓▓▓▓▓ my entire apartment, embarked on some short-lived ▓▓▓▓▓▓▓▓▓▓, founded a ▓▓▓▓▓ with an amazing ▓▓▓▓▓ and pulled together a book.

I also approached the nine-month postponement of my surgery as a kind of "pregnancy." The idea of giving birth to my own vagina is a very "me" way of looking at things and it was quite helpful in giving me a framework to cope with the devastating last-minute loss of my first attempt.

This time around, though, I have a growing feeling that I'm going to be devastated. For real. I'm not getting any younger and while I quite like the hot cougar vibe I have grown into, cougars need to prowl. Also, the fact I am not getting younger makes post-surgical recovery that much more daunting.

I am having a harder and harder time looking at a photo like this one and repressing the fact that I am without vaj. It is exhausting to have to mentally photoshop the existence of the silly little useless caterpillar between my legs out of my consciousness day after day after day. I have Big P energy--the P does not rhyme with "Venus" BTW--and the inability to express that outside of manically taking photos and ▓▓▓▓▓▓▓▓▓▓ and writing books is really getting to me.

I blacked out the plot points that are about to unfold as I would hate to ruin the joy of discovery for you. I don't think the book is a secret anymore, so we'll let that one stand. Back to my vagina, though. This is as good a place as any to talk a little bit more about it's importance to me. You may be surprised.

Transitioning is a lot of work. Like, it's a hell of a lot more than just swapping out one sex hormone for another, and THAT is a pretty big undertaking all on its own, let me tell you. Everything related to the induction of a second puberty is what we call the Medical Transition, and just like the first puberty, it's a wild ride. Body fat moves around. You lose hair in places, gain it in others. For many transitioning from

testosterone to estrogen, you may even lose some fluid in your spine and feet, so it's possible to drop a little height and a shoe size or two. For reals. Your neurological map begins to rewire in response to running on a different fuel and you experience emotions and sensations in different ways.

Alongside all that fun stuff with the body and mind, there is the Social Transition, which entails things like changing your name and your drivers license and your gender marker on all official documents and making sure the credit reporting agencies update their records and changing all your bank and financial documents and hoping that when you walk up to the cashier at the grocery store in a dress you don't get called "sir" and that when in mixed company nobody refers to you as "he" and AHHHHHHHHHH it's a lot!

Notice that in discussing various medical and social elements of my transition I didn't say a word about my genitals. On the nearly-infinitely long Transition To-Do list that I have been working through, bottom surgery has always been in last place as a priority. Always. I was determined to step into the world and be accepted as myself without having to pass an Innie/Outie test and that is exactly what I have done. Others may have a different set of priorities and that is great for them, but this is my path. I decided to take the Smith Barney approach, and I pray there is at least one person out there who gets that reference. Just one. Whoever you are, please send me an email or something.

The obsession with genitals that trans-skeptic, trans-hostile, and trans-phobic people have is bizarre. Unless we are on a train to Funville, Climaxtown, or St. Orgasmus, then I have ZERO interest in what is between your legs, and I would ask that you not express any interest in what is between mine.

Every single time there is a story about a trans person in the news, I go straight to the comments section to check my assumptions about the persistent ignorance that remains in society about the trans identity. "God created Adam and Eve" and "Chromosomes don't lie" and "Still a dude" are there every single time. It's like people are too lazy to say anything else and just cut and paste the same tired lines over and over.

If you happen to be one of those kinds of people and are reading these words, then I have two messages for you. First: thanks for buying my book! Second, I am very confident that somewhere out there, Jesus is doing backflips while high-fiving a unicorn over my existence. God created me as well. It took a little longer than six days, but here I am in all Their glory.

Now where is that Mic? I think it needs to be dropped.

S3E2 | Cassandra is Right Where She is Supposed to Be

This pic on the left is from one year ago 'after' I came out, after I went full dose, after I started to expect people to treat me as the woman who was finally emerging. I look at it now, though, and it seems so 'before' in countless ways. . .

Before I got control of my body. Before I got used to my name. Before my curves appeared. Before I went from wondering if people would ever accept me to expecting that they would accept me to not caring whether they accept me or not because I know they will. Before a LOT of change that has taken place over the past year.

I do want to acknowledge, though, that I am very conflicted about sharing these 'before' pics. They are very triggering for me. Not just from a vain, narcissistic perspective, but also because I still deal with dysphoria, still have moments where I wonder if my inner light shines through.

I still believe that it's valuable to share them, though, because they do a singular job of illustrating what a transition looks like, and that is the reason why I post, to share this experience with anyone who is interested.

But seriously. Holy shit.

#bethechangeyouwanttoseeintheworld

#transformationtuesday #transproud

#transitiontuesday

Not a lot to say here beyond the several thousand words that these two photos already convey. I will add just a few more though. In fact, there is one that I would like to emphasize: energy.

There are countless metrics that I can apply to measure the changes that have taken place. Skin tone. Hip size. Voice pitch. Comfort at calling one of my girlfriends "Bitch" and meaning it as a term of endearment. And on and on and on.

I look at a lot of photos taken after I began my social transition—like the one on the left here—and it is very easy for me to focus on some of those metrics and wonder why people ever called me "Ma'am" and "Miss" and "Your Ladyship." Hell, I look at some of the photos I have included in this book and I can pick them apart with ruthless precision. That's the moment where I start to wonder if, in spite of the artistic license I have allowed myself here, I am not simply the central character in a Truman Show-esque fantasyland in which the Universe around me exists to humor my self-delusion.

The conclusion that I come to again and again, though, the one that gives me reassurance that this is all actually happening is that the only metric that really matters is energy. People see my energy, they feel my womanhood, and the rest flows from that.

Ok...I know that last sentence has some issues, but since I don't have to worry about an actual editor for this book, I'm going to leave it in because it makes me chuckle. Actually, I don't chuckle anymore. I snort. My doctor didn't tell me that my laugh would change, but here we are.

The evolution of my presentation has been gradual, but the expression of my energy was instantaneous, like flipping a switch. The moment I committed to transitioning, I committed. Like, all the way. I continue to have fun using fashion as a medium of self-expression, continue to discover new forms of presentation, but the turning point in my acceptance by others was the moment when I accepted myself and allowed my inner light to shine through. Apparently it burns rather brightly.

S3E3 | Cassandra Paints Her Apartment

Did I mention that I painted my bedroom purple? And my bathroom yellow?

Thoughts?

#quarantinelife #ilovemybody

#thesubtleartofnotgivingafuck

#bikiniseason

It may be difficult to tell, but I was growing increasingly confident in my body. Also probably not that apparent, but I had ridiculous amounts of pent-up sexual energy. I know, right? If I hadn't said something, how would you have noticed? Since I had no real constructive outlet for all this energy, I took lots and lots of photos of myself making love to my selfie camera. The "lower lip hanging down, drool about to come pouring out" look in that one shot was a staple of this period.

A lot of these photos made their way onto Instagram. Many others, especially those that would have violated Instagram's rather strict content restrictions, made their way to gentleman admirers around the world who were struggling to make it through the darkest days of quarantine. I am nothing if not a humanitarian.

All those mistakes you make in your twenties and thirties? The ones you worry about showing up on a review of your social media activity when you apply for that job you really want? I never made any of them, so I decided to take advantage of the remote learning opportunity that quarantine provided and make them all at once.

I knew that if I were to ever function sexually as a woman in the real world, then I would need to learn how to handle the intense objectification and commodification of my body that had suddenly become a huge part of my life. So while I was all undressed with nowhere to go, I resolved to teach myself a Graduate Degree in Setting Boundaries with a Minor Concentration in Flirting.

Every comment on my body, every proposition in a DM, every conversation that I had while sitting in that bathtub and weighing whether the person on the other end deserved to receive a photo or two from The Vault; these were all invaluable experiences in helping me better understand and manage the relentless energy that is the male libido.

About that. While I may have been born with a caterpillar that responded to various forms of stimulation, I have never, ever, EVER had a male libido. Being on the receiving end of male sexual energy is all the confirmatory evidence I need that I never possessed any of my own. OMG, you guys are animals!

The most memorable experience I had during my self-study period was when I was managing four separate conversations with four different guys, having made the mistake of sending them all the exact same photo. Each chat went off into a different direction based on the personality of the guy, and I had to keep all that stuff organized in my head. What was so intense about this you ask? All four conversations were happening at the same time. Talk about multi-tasking!

Also, please take note of that Bubble Bath Bikini photo. Little did I know, but it would end up playing a fairly significant role in one of the sub-plots that take place in Season Four.

S3E4 | Cassandra Tries to Keep it Real

As I start to think about meeting people in real life who only know me through my online 'persona'—whether its friends or future spouses—I'm really starting to freak out over pictures like this one.

Whether I objectively look like this or not, I have NEVER in my life taken pictures that look like this. Just the pictures alone represent a massive change in my appearance.

But how 'real' are they? Heads up on what may sound like the world's least self-aware comment, but roll with me on this. I often get asked: 'How do you look so good?' My response is always the same: 'I don't! I just take tons of pics and post the few that are hot.'

I look back on my body of work here from time to time (who am I kidding—I'm so self-absorbed I look at it ALL the time) and I have to say, it's really impressive how many different looks I'm pulling off. It's also really intimidating because I don't know if I can live up to this in the flesh. In fact, I know I can't.

I also know that the only way to deal with fear is to confront it head-on, so with much nervous anticipation I'm hoping to meet some people who only know me from my online presence. I'm totally prepared for them to take one look at me—or one listen to my hideous voice—and say 'nah, I'm good' while thinking 'what a fraud' as they walk away.

I know that's just another experience I have to go through to keep growing and settling into a place of genuine confidence about the real, non-Instagram me. In the meantime, enjoy this pic of someone who, I gotta say, I would totally do in a heartbeat.

#insecure #vulnerability #humblebrag

#steppingout #keepingitreal

This photo came around the time when I was beginning to ramp up Operation Embrace the Unicorn, what I decided to call my experiment with dating after the cancellation of my bottom surgery. What I meant by this was that I would put myself out there as is, i.e., caterpillar and all, and see if any sparks fly. One thing I was 100% adamant about, however, was that nobody would actually be embracing my unicorn.

Blessings and good tidings to every person who is comfortable with their body in whatever configuration it might be. Particularly warm wishes to all of the "equipment is equipment" people out there who take a "whole of person" approach to being with someone. I mean that. I'm not being sarcastic. I've been told it's hard to tell sometimes, hence the clarification. I, however, am not an "equipment is equipment" person, at least as far as the equipment that I have been waiting my entire life to have properly installed.

I remember the first time I got aroused. Like, the first time I have a conscious memory of it. I was nine or so, lying in bed, not really touching anything, and then all of a sudden, things started to feel very, uh, interesting down there. In fact, I was afraid to touch anything because I didn't want to ruin what was happening. It was good! But I also remember what was going on in my head.

There was a fairy that appeared and turned me into a woman. The transformation was total, and it allowed me to enjoy the moment playing out in my head with no shame, no guilt, and no inhibition. And no, I had not seen Tinkerbell turn one of the Lost Boys into a girl on The Wonderful World of Disney the Sunday before. This was just how my brain processed arousal: it knew I was a woman and therefore processed these feelings in the only way it could make sense of them.

Ever since, whatever the outer packaging, whatever the shell, one thing that has been 100% unwaveringly consistent my entire life is who I am at the moment of orgasm. I know how all the various pieces fall into place for the key to smoothly enter the lock and open the door to Good Times. I also know how much effort I have had to spend in the past finding ways to stitch together the tremendous gulf between mind and body just long enough to feel release. I'm tired of that effort.

To paraphrase one of the greats, one does not simply walk into a surgeon's office and receive a vagina. Getting approval for bottom surgery is an arduous process that involves multiple letters of referral from medical and psychological professionals who follow rigorous standards.

Ever the inquisitive mind, I asked one of the people who was reviewing my case if there were any themes or trends that she has noticed over the years with how people respond after the procedure. She told me that one thing she heard over and over was that people just felt a wave of relief from a stress that they had been carrying their whole lives, that the relief was unexpected because the stress had simply been internalized: it was all they ever knew.

This book is many things, but it is not a tell-all, so I am not going to tell all about some of my experiences. I will say this in sum about Operation Embrace the Unicorn, however: it didn't take me long to realize that the juice was not worth the squeeze.

The bottom line is that I drew a bottom line at my waist beyond which I did not want anyone to go and it quickly got frustrating to be the driver taking someone else to Pleasureville. I have needs beyond the emotional validation of being desired, and since they weren't going to be met, I was basically done.

Overall, though, it was a really positive experience. In order to help bridge the gap between persona and person that growing up on Instagram had created, I needed people to see me in motion, listen to my voice, and feel my skin. My focus group was diverse, I was rigorous in asking the tough questions, and I got the feedback I needed inside of a few weeks. I didn't need to replicate the experiment a hundred times if I was confident in what the result would be after just a few. Ok, more than just a few.

Also, this was all happening during the initial stages of the pandemic. So there was the whole "if I keep on doing this there is a greater and greater chance that I could die or inadvertently kill someone" element that factored into my risk-reward calculus.

I talk a little bit more about my decision to close up shop in Season Four, because my experiences on the dating scene were formative in where I decided to redirect all of this smoldering sexual energy. Spoiler alert: if I were all set downstairs, you would probably not be reading this book.

S3E5 | Cassandra Comes Out of the Shadows

Today is #transitiontuesday and while I have posted my fair share of 'Then and Now' pictures, no picture I've ever taken does a better job of conveying my relationship to my transition than this one.

Undeniably the person who is in focus here is, well, yeah: kinda hot. That's the person that you all see, the one I let you see because of the pictures that I choose to show. Behind that person, though, is a looming shadow. That's the shadow of my dysphoria.

Most days, like in this picture, the shadow recedes to the background and you might not even notice it, especially if you are looking at my boobs. But for me it's always there, always. And there are still days when I get lost in that shadow, when I am convinced that my body is as large as the one haunting me in this picture, my features as blandly masculine as the silhouette that stalks me, my femininity just a trick of angles and clothes and makeup.

Wherever you are in your journey, whatever your deal, let's all keep each other in focus and do our best to not let anyone—our friends, our family, ourselves—slip too far back into the shadows.

#thisiswhattranslookslike #girlslikeus

#transformationtuesday #bethechange

There are a lot of aspects to mind-body alignment that I am still figuring out as my body continues to evolve. One of the challenging things I get to unpack on any given day is how much of my perception of myself is warped because I am transitioning, and how much because I am aging. How much is my body changing because of things I can control like diet and exercise, and how much is it changing because of things I can't, like gravity and time. These are factors that anyone conscious of their appearance may care about. I care about all of them, all the time.

In other news, this is by far my favorite photo of my shoulder tattoo as it best illustrates its multiple layers of meaning.

The original tattoo, which you can see in this B&W shot, is a tribal Superman design. It was the first tattoo I ever got and...do I even need to break this down for anyone? The motivation behind the tattoo, the symbolism of it all? Just embarrassing levels of cliché and overcompensation here on display. Where is that "facepalm" emoji when I need it?

As almost all good ideas are wont to do, the vision to cover it up with a butterfly came to me in the shower. I had known for a while that I wanted a butterfly tattoo because, well, one could probably say "embarrassing levels of cliché" and I would grant you that, but "overcompensation" not so much.

Anyway, the idea was to use the original design as the foundation and then cover it up completely with the butterfly. I love the color, I love the boldness of it, and I love that it fails to completely cover up the original tattoo. I love that these two symbols could not be more extreme in what they represent, but that they come together and represent a harmonious synthesis of my identity.

S3E6 | Cassandra's Greek Odyssey

I cannot get enough of this Mediterranean fantasy of an outfit from Roman and my new favorite pair of earrings from Adornia.

My love for Roman is pretty well established here—the majority of my 'OMG THAT LOOKS AMAZING' outfits are from them— but I also proudly consider myself an #adorniawoman and effing adore these ssssnake earrings I just picked up.

You know who else likes Adornia? That's right, @brookeshields . So that makes TWO things she and I have in common. The other one? Well, I promised not to tell, but his secret is safe with us.

#greekgoddess #fashionista

All I am going to say in response to this post is that if I ever really wanted to do the Fashionista/Influencer thing full-time, I would totally crush it. I mean, this is a TEXTBOOK example of how to Instagram.

Aside from that, just the very idea that I was doing something like this is insane to me, given how I spent the vast majority of my life. Insane. Like, Lifetime Achievement Award levels of insane. Zero to Fashionista in six months flat.

S3E7 | Cassandra is on Top of the World

This is a post about boobs. Eyes down here, please.

For the longest time I never thought that top surgery was a possibility for me. I worried it would invalidate my transition in the eyes of others. "Oh, she went and got bigger boobs to 'prove' how much of a woman she is" I feared people would think.

Spoiler alert: I know what's wrong with that thinking—we'll get there in a bit.

As I spoke over the past year to more and more of my girlfriends—some trans, many not— who have had Breast Augmentation, I kept hearing the exact same thing: 'best decision I ever made.' Did not matter who I was talking to or when they had their surgery, it was thumbs up all around.

I started to ask myself why I had to be different, what I actually feared. The turning point came last October when I attended a fashion show for breast cancer awareness. Every single woman who walked was a survivor, they all had BA, and they were glorious, absolutely glorious. Nobody doubted their authentic femininity for a second.

Sitting there I asked myself 'Am I any less of a woman than they are?' And since I'm not, I realized how afraid I was of being judged and how much I was ceding control of my body to others' perceptions of me. Once I realized that, it was a no-brainer to move forward.

I had a consultation a few months ago and the moment I held the implants up to my chest, I felt them fuse right into me. I had planned on starting with bottom surgery and waiting for the cherries on top until later, but since V-Day got postponed until next year, I'm going forward with BA this August. Scheduled it yesterday.

I'm sharing this for the same reason I've shared all the other details of my transition over the past six months: it's all part of my journey and if you are THAT person who needs to hear this, it is my absolute honor to be a messenger for you. Anyone else: enjoy this hot pic of my already pretty sweet boobs.

#gendereuphoria #mybodymychoice #grownasswoman #soymilk

Some of my photos are the result of intricately staged shoots. I will spend an entire evening going through different outfits and different lighting and different bottles of wine until I am happy with the results.

Not this photo.

I remember taking this photo right before I headed out to Target. I thought I looked kind of Trans Wine Mom hot and wanted to capture the moment. When I looked at it and saw that I was rocking some pretty tight Cherry Garcia-fueled cleavage, though, I knew I would use the photo to make the announcement that I had scheduled top surgery. You know, because bewbs.

That's all this post was at the time: me just talking openly about my body, freely sharing details of my journey, one that I was clearly enjoying. As I look at it now, though, I see it as a marker of a significant change in my life, of a branching path that I had never gone down before.

I was developmentally at a point in my transition where I was stepping into young adulthood and I could see how incredibly different it was unfolding this time around. Like, that part about becoming an adult where you forget about your hopes and dreams and just resign yourself to a lifetime of doing what others expect of you? Yeah, this time not so much.

OMG!! Did transitioning turn me into a Millennial?

S3E8 | Cassandra Meets Her Match

I can't be the only one thinking that these two should totally make out with each other, right?

#justasking #problemsolved #selflove

There is self-love. There is self-absorption. Then there is this. Of all the Hollywood properties I've suggested remaking, it's taken me this long to finally see the potential that is SCREAMING at me from these two photos.

Imagine the John Travolta/Nick Cage classic "Face-Off", but as a genderfluid romantic comedy where the surgical exchange doesn't happen with the faces, but rather...

WHAT?! Am I really the only one that thinks that is a pretty interesting concept for a movie? Perhaps this is why Hollywood has yet to option any of my ideas.

Anyway...

It was March of 2019 when I came out as trans, got my first bloodwork showing zero testosterone and a normal level of estrogen for a woman my age, and decided to up my estrogen to what is considered a full "transition" dose. As you can see in that photo on the left, 47 years of testosterone had done quite a number on me. While my inner light was shining through and I was living my truth and all that good stuff, I could still pull off "moderately attractive fella" with ease.

I'm not smiling in that pic, though, because I'm sexy and I know it. I'm smiling because I'm so relieved that my second puberty was underway and that my body was catching up to where my mind had already been for some time.

A lot of the 'Transition Tuesday' photos underscore how stark the changes are that have taken place, to include the journey from "miserable wretch" to "blossoming flower." As powerful and instructive and cathartic as those photographic juxtapositions can be, they only show the extreme end of the spectrum many of us travel. Photos like these two, however, tell a different story. In my case, they highlight the evolutionary journey that I am on, as well as my enjoyment of it as it is taking place.

In case anyone is thinking it, let me add that I know very well that if I had stopped around May 2019 and enjoyed the Benjamin Button effect going on here, that I could have spent the next twenty to thirty years pulling all kinds of action. That's just not who I am, though. Not at all. It does weird me out, however, when my girlfriends see photos of what I looked like before and tell me without a moment's hesitation how hot I was and, in some cases, how much they would have liked to have slept with me. Yeah. This happens. It happens a lot.

On the one hand, I take this as a pretty solid piece of confirmatory validation that they now view me as one of the girls and are lusting after "him" as if it were just another guy we were chatting about. On the other hand, WHAT THE FUCK?!?!

These kinds of comments really weird me out and I still don't fully understand what is behind them. I am, however, now thinking about how we can fold this dynamic into the movie pitch I mentioned above.

MAY 2019   MAY 2020

BRA PIC 2019   BRA PIC 2020

S3E9 | Cassandra Suspects the Estrogen Might be Working

Pic on the left is from exactly one year ago. I had been on a full dose of HRT for three months and just begun my short-lived 'Trans Who Fell to Earth' hair homage to Bowie.

Pic on the right is from, uh, now. Apparently that's what I look like. I've got another 500 pics on my phone to back that up. That would be 500 pics from Sunday.

#gendereuphoria #mybodymychoice

#grownasswoman #soymilk

I would love to talk about the all the differences that these two photos represent. About the physical changes that are evident such as the thickness and density of my hair, the results of another year of taking care of my skin (and finally using sunscreen!!!), and the fact that in both of these photos I am too freaking skinny.

I'd love to talk about the growing confidence in my femininity that is clearly visible and the differences in the kind of energy that I am projecting. About the shift from an almost demure "Oh, look, a camera!" innocence on the left to the absurdly over-the-top "Do me, NOW!" vibe I'm giving off on the right.

There is an interesting discussion to be had about the wisdom of a middle-aged parent of three grown children who has extraordinarily ambitious professional aspirations putting these kinds of photos on social media. I mean, we can talk about the wisdom of it all day long, but the photos are there and, oh, they are here as well, so the "wisdom" piece of that discussion is pretty academic at this point. But still, we could talk about it.

But I don't really want to talk about any of that. I just want to pause and admire that eye shadow game. OMFG is that amazing and how in the hell did I ever do that? Like, I don't even know what palette that is. I think it's one of my Smashbox palettes but honestly, since I switched over to the Laura Mercier Caviar Stick Eye Shadow (obsessed!) I don't even know if I could still pull this off.

Like the joy of navigating with a paper map, I fear this is a skill that may forever be lost to the past.

S3E10 | Cassandra Gives a Litmus Test

Dear Followers: if you are open-minded, compassionate, and actively anti-racist, please enjoy these pictures of me as a badass biker chick.

If you are anything less than that, if you are wondering what the big deal is, why people are burning down city blocks, why rage is flowing in the streets of America, then please fuck right off.

Yes, this is an Instagram about my experiences as a middle-aged trans woman and my love affair with my selfie camera. It is not about the institutional racism in the US that murdered George Floyd and countless others over the centuries.

Spoiler Alert: If you don't think the US is institutionally racist, then you are part of the institution that is racist. This is not up for debate.

But for anyone with a platform of any kind, whether that's a couple thousand followers on Instagram or your immediate friends and family, your coworkers, your partner (or partners, 'cause there's a lot of that out there), silence in reaction to injustice is not only a form of consent, but a form of cowardice as well.

So please speak up, act up, act out, do ANYTHING but stay silent in the face of this enduring evil.

#fightthepower #bethechange

#transpride #transwoman

So day after day after day on Instagram, everyone is having a pretty good time telling each other how awesome we all are. Some of us post photos with captions that are derived from random word generators, often using the most minute variations of the same photo over and over. Others use the platform as a creative sandbox and an environment to beta test the application of insights gleaned from therapy. To each her own. All in all, though, we post our content, pat each other on the back, and then call it a day. Then we get up and do it again. And again.

Then George Floyd gets murdered and millions and millions of people watch him get murdered on social media and the reality of the world beyond your ring light is impossible to ignore.

I am proud of everything that I put in this book. I am not any more or less proud of these posts on racial injustice than I am of any other in here for the simple reason that they all represent who I am. I'm not looking for any bonus points for taking the only morally defensible stand in response to these events.

I aim for these reflective texts to provide additional context for the posts that I originally put on Instagram, not to defend them or rationalize them or guard against certain kinds of interpretations. Those posts are out there, they are part of my historical record, and taken as a whole, they represent my life. But also my art. For me, those two words are fully synonymous, and while this may look like a performance to some, there is nothing performative about it.

S3E11 | Cassandra Asks for Pride in the Name of Love

Care about what's going on in the US with race but don't yet want to burn something down? Here is something you can do—RIGHT NOW—to make a difference.

Companies are starting to post about what is going on. Many are doing a fantastic job of taking a stand and announcing action. Their Instas are being flooded with comments both supportive and hostile.

Look, it's Pride month. Whatever you think of all the rainbow-themed junk corporations peddle during June, it's a stone-cold fact that this has helped to make the other eleven months of the year a little safer and welcoming for us queer folk. If you are queer, then no matter how hard your current situation is, no matter what you think of corporations, it is a fact that support for Pride has created positive social change for us. It's a fact.

Additionally, as someone who has partnered with companies like Sephora, Anthropologie, Roman USA, Lululemon, and some others I'll announce down the road, I 100% stand behind the power of corporate advocacy. It's why I think we should be flooding the Instas of companies right now and either lauding them for taking concrete stands to address racial injustice or pressuring them to do so if they are not.

Please hop on these posts and applaud these companies for the positions they are taking. Whether you like it or not, money

talks and if it can be leveraged for what we think is good, then let's encourage these companies to do the right thing.

I'm telling you, based on what I've seen the past hour, some of them are getting slammed for announcing these initiatives. Maybe take some time and offer positive, encouraging feedback to these companies to help this grow into an even stronger movement. Ignore the haters, cause haters gonna hate, but make some positive noise and maybe this will take root.

Pressure on corporations helped end Apartheid in South Africa. As corporate as Pride has become, its existence makes my life safer. Speaking up doesn't always have to mean shouting someone down. Here it can mean telling someone they are doing a good job and helping to change the tide of what values we want to have as a society.

To everyone with a platform: please get back in the game. 'Stepping aside to let other voices be heard' is noble, but you have a voice that needs to be heard and that can contribute positively. Right now. Please don't cede the work to those who have been doing it all along. It just creates more for them.

#pride #inthenameoflove
#speakup #makeadifference
#lovewins #getinthegame

Testosterone is a reactive hormone. It just is. I'm not breaking any new scientific ground here. Couple its reactiveness with all that self-loathing, and you've got a pretty potent recipe for unpleasant vibes. Thankfully, for myself and others, my entire emotional range has changed as a result of transitioning. Part of it, a large part to be sure, is the whole "no-longer-loathing-myself" thing. But a lot of it is the hormonal fuel that I am running on.

Understanding this has been a process.

I remember the first time I got sad after beginning my transition. I totally freaked out: OH NO, IT'S NOT WORKING ANYMORE!!! And then I realized that "sad" is an emotion that I am allowed to have, that non-stop 24/7 euphoria is not a normal—nor healthy—state of being. So I allowed sad into my emotional toolbox, over time appreciating nuances in how differently I now experience it. Sad generally feels the same as it used to, but it doesn't last nearly as long and it never turns to anger.

Speaking of anger, I barely recognized it when I first felt it because of how different it now looks. Like, this post, these photos, this is a pretty good representation of what my "rage" looks like now. It's pretty intense, no?

I'm writing these words in mid-December 2020. Thanks to the internet there really is no such thing as an outdated reference anymore, so I can drop the following anecdote with confidence that if you don't know what the hell I am talking about, this section is only a Google search away from making sense.

Anyway, last night I got distracted from my work on the book by the "Tom Cruise Screaming On The Set of Mission Impossible" story. In case you missed it, TC went ballistic over some crew members not following COVID protocols and proceeded to scream at them for a few minutes (maybe more, but the recording was only a few minutes long) over the risk they were presenting to the livelihood of thousands of people and to the very future of the movie industry.

I listened to that recording and my reaction was immediate: "Wow, that's what I used to sound like."

I'm not saying Tom Cruise loathes himself, nor am I saying that he should hop on board the E-train and see how he responds. All I'm saying is that if the Illuminati want to put something else into the water above and beyond the fluoride, they could do a lot worse than estrogen.

For the record, I do know the difference between the Illuminati and Scientology. One is a secretive cabal that believes in made-up nonsense and has messianic aspirations to control the world, while the other is the group that Beyoncé runs. Duh.

I've always been principled, always been opinionated, always been a bit of a pain in the ass, the squeaky wheel, the loudmouth.

What I am just at the very beginning of appreciating, though, is how all of those things that I have always been are now filtered through the prism of my transition. There are a lot of things that I felt or thought but never had the ability to express. Or I may have expressed them, but rarely in a way that connected positively with others.

Regardless of the purity of the principle on which I was standing, the righteousness of my cause was often eclipsed by the rage in my voice. For example, however much I was trying to keep the interconnected web of the universe from fraying because my daughter's wet towel was left on her bedroom floor, my message never really got through. I'm pretty sure it was because of how angrily I was delivering it. I'm sorry, my dear, I really am.

S3E12 | Cassandra Talks Abou
Pride and Prejudice

This period marked a turning point for me in my relationship with the trans community. This was the first community that I had ever really felt a part of and I was quite sad to feel less and less connected to it the longer I spent on Instagram. It took me 47 years to embrace being transgender and when I did, I felt a wave of relief to know that I wasn't actually broken, wasn't a perpetual outcast, and that there were others I could connect with from a position of shared experience. After feeling alone and shunned and one of the misfit toys for so long, it was an amazing relief to find an online island where we all fit in.

When the protests in the US broke out, people on Instagram with platforms reacted in different ways. Some people just stopped posting. Like, the party is over and please let me know when it's ok to come back. Others continued to post as if nothing had changed. Of course, Instagram is a global community, so you had people from the rest of the world keep on keeping on, one day wondering why so many people in the US were posting a black square.

Like several of the posts I did around this time, this was more of a statement of my own values than anything else. But it was also a reaction to a lot of what I was seeing, a lot that I didn't feel comfortable participating in anymore.

I don't want to tell anyone how they should run their platform, what they should say, how they should feel. "Should" is such a loaded word and I try and avoid it. I'm just putting my voice out there and if you like it, great, if you don't, that's also fine.

This was me at peak preachy and having said my peace, I started to make some "peace out" decisions as to how much effort I wanted to spend engaging with certain kinds of platforms.

S3E13

Cassandra Wonders Whether She is Trans

I've been thinking a lot lately about whether I'm trans. I'm obviously transgender—duh—but what I mean by 'trans' is the community, it's norms and culture. Oddly, I've felt that the longer I've been living openly as a transgender woman, the less connected I am to the trans community. Both here on Instagram as well as in the real world.

I wear my transgender identity with tremendous pride. Like, the first line of my dating profile says: "Intensely hungry and proud AF trans woman who knows her worth and is curious about yours." I applied for a new job recently and I spent a couple paragraphs in my application talking about how my experience being transgender makes me that much more qualified for the position.

I don't pass and have never tried to pass in the sense of not wanting someone to know that I'm transgender. It's obvious that I am, and since I can't hide it, I might as well own it. And I don't WANT to hide it because I think this experience is a blessing not a curse, regardless of how hard it's been and how much I've lost along the way.

It seems, though, that there are two dominant narratives in the trans experience: the Struggle Narrative and the Joy Narrative. Maybe what I'm feeling is that Joy is an individual journey while Struggle is something that brings people together. I celebrate my Joy pretty regularly, even though the Struggle has been very real and remains so. Maybe that celebration is alienating?

#thisiswhattranslookslike

#fashionblogger #transwoman

#legsfordays #leatherjacket

"Passing" in the trans community has traditionally meant not being clocked as trans, i.e., nobody knowing your origin story. Someone sees you and it never enters into their head that you are trans. That's the simplest, most straightforward definition of what passing has meant. As more and more trans people live openly and proudly in society, though, it is coming to mean a broad spectrum of things, to include meaning nothing at all.

On the one hand, I know girls who are proudly, defiantly trans, who literally wrap themselves in the trans flag and assert their womanhood with a fierce disdain for any of the norms of beauty culture. Passing in the above sense is not a goal and plays no part in the validity of their identity. I know girls who live stealth, who have made every effort to pass and are terrified of someone finding out that they are trans. I also know girls who have made every effort to pass and who are proudly and openly trans. Like I said, a broad spectrum.

For the longest time, though, passing was the ultimate goal. The Netflix documentary "Disclosure" does a good job of discussing the significance of passing by showing how trans people have traditionally been portrayed by Hollywood. Sidebar: watching this movie is a "wonderful" lesson in why anyone growing up trans prior to, say, 2018 has had to deal with all kinds of internalized self-loathing about their identity.

I don't know where I fit in on the above spectrum, if I do at all. And at this point, I don't think it matters. Going stealth was never an option for me because I never wanted it to be an option. I was always intent on bending the world to accept me instead of bending for the world's acceptance. Since I can pull off "Barbie Basic Bitch" pretty well, I'm just going to ride that wave for as long as I can and see where it takes me.

To my delight, though, I'm finding that the longer I exist openly in the world as a woman, the more I am realizing that so many issues connected to my appearance are about that, and not about the fact that I am trans. Mind you, there are things I have to deal with that are unique to me being trans. Having a caterpillar inconveniently attached to my crotch as opposed to a butterfly is one of those things.

But there are also a lot more things that I have to deal with that I THOUGHT were unique to me being trans but are actually just part of the joy of being a woman. The size of my breasts, for example. The moment I realized that this had nothing to do with me being trans but everything to do with me being a woman was a huge moment of relief. One less trans thing to worry about!

I say all this because I know that when it comes to beauty culture, the Venn Diagram of Trans Women and Non-Trans Women is an almost perfect eclipse. From body image concerns to eating disorders, cosmetic procedures to hair removal, we all deal with this stuff, some of it more pressing than others depending on the numbers we drew in the genetic lottery, or how much we care about what the person working the checkout at Whole Foods thinks about our eyelashes.

S3E14 | Cassandra Gets Admitted to the Barre

A favor, my friends...

I am very, very proud to be featured today on Pure Barre in their message of solidarity with Pride.

I wrote a text about what Pure Barre has meant to my transition and it is over on their Insta. If you are curious, please check it out.

My favor is to ask you to consider sharing that post to help spread this Good News Story of inclusion for the trans community. It is merely one story, and many more need to be written for many communities, but it does represent a step forward and every step counts.

#pridemonth #fitwoman

#purebarre #transvisibility

I feel quite strongly that there are universally-applicable principles of managing change in a gradual, intentional, and incremental way that anyone can apply to any kind of "transition" in their own life, whatever the context. I feel strongly about that because I have been in the Change Management space for many years, helping others map out and then follow step-by-step roadmaps to bring about lasting change. Ironic, no? And truly ironic, not in a "rain on your wedding day" kind of way.

So it shouldn't be a surprise that when I finally got around to managing my own change, I applied many of those same principles to myself. More about this shocking development in Season Four.

One thing I did not do, however, was come up with a clear vision or defined end state for how I should look. My overarching goal in starting hormones was to reduce the pain I was experiencing because of the mind/body airgap. That was it. I hit that milestone early on, and the rest has been a series of expanding horizons as I firm up the ground under my feet.

It sounds kind of dismissive and unserious to say that I am making this up as I go along—because I'm not—but there is an element of adaptive improvisation at play as I let my inner light shine brighter and brighter and set my sights higher and higher.

And in a nutshell—no pun intended, I swear—this sums up the evolutionary approach I have taken in managing what is a pretty revolutionary change when taken as a whole. Day after day I stepped toward challenge after challenge, cauterizing myself against fear and insecurity and hostility by pushing deeper and deeper into newer and newer experiences. Something, something, follow your dreams, amirite?

Of all the spaces where I've earned my place, my approach to Pure Barre is the best example of what I just described. Putting in the work class after class, overcoming my fears bit by bit, and seeing the lasting change in my body has been one of the greatest joys and greatest accomplishments of my transition.

When it comes to confronting fear and stepping into adversity and all that, though, I do want to make clear that I am not a reckless dumbass who thinks she is invincible. I went to pick up kebabs the other day and there were four loud, obnoxious dudes sitting outside making all kinds of noise and generally giving off the vibes of people looking to take a verbal dump on someone. I was wearing my workout clothes and super tight leggings, so I decided to walk up to where they were sitting and wait until someone made an offensive comment about my appearance so that I could teach them a lesson.

Of course I didn't do that! As soon as that little "stranger danger" alarm went off, I calculated my every step to make sure I minimized the potential for any one of them to notice me. I'm not looking to invite unnecessary "growth experiences" into my life.

It's one thing to be afraid to go to the pool in a bikini, another thing to walk to my car at night in a mostly empty parking lot and wonder if the guy sitting in the oversized pick-up truck parked next to me is going to make a move before I can get in and lock my doors.

Come to think of it, that also happened when I went to get kebabs. Ok, lesson learned: I think I should stop getting kebabs.

This is what my transition looks like. It's #pridemonth and I'm proud AF that I'm trans, so let's get real.

I exist in the world as the woman on the right. Whatever I look like to you, hot or not, more or less feminine depending on the angle, lighting, outfit, etc., I exist in the world as a woman. Period.

Well, maybe not the period. Kinda missed out on that whole experience and I will count that as a blessing. But I digress.

I'm super uncomfortable sharing this kind of a picture these days, but not because I worry that anyone will look at me and see him. This picture freaks me out because I look at him and see someone who has passed away.

There is trauma in that. I experience trauma in the awareness of having brought the existence of that person on the left to an end. There is trauma in having the memories of someone who existed in the world as a man echoing around my head as if they were uploaded, copied and pasted over from a person I, Cassandra, never really was and most definitely no longer am.

There is also joy and euphoria and liberation in experiencing what feels like rebirth, like literal reincarnation. The awareness of that, of how unique the gift of transitioning is, makes all this effort, all the struggle worthwhile.

Man/Woman, Adam/Eve, Penis/Vagina: gender as an assumed iron-clad binary permeates how we see the world and how the world sees us. To transcend that, to be given the gift of re-experiencing the world through a completely different paradigm, one that finally aligns with who I am....it's nothing short of a mother-forking miracle.

Also, fun fact: the picture on the left was taken three years ago. I had just started talking to my therapist about accepting that I was trans and asking what could be done about it. I was inspired to take action because of pictures like these. As traumatic as it is for me to look at this, I hope it can help someone who needs to see this to inspire them to change, whatever that may look like.

#thisiswhattranslookslike #bethechange

#transitiontuesday #hrt #transwoman

S3E15 | Cassandra Splits The Difference

There are a lot of aspects of my transition that are surprisingly relatable. Yeah, it's a pretty extreme expression of change, but everybody changes in different ways throughout their life and when seen through that lens, I'm able to connect with all kinds of people who see my transition as merely an extreme example of something they have experienced. Moving to another country, changing jobs, getting divorced, losing a lot of weight, etc., etc., and on and on. These are all "transitions" of some sort and there are mechanisms of successfully navigating change that apply to all of them.

Even the whole "second puberty" thing. Ok, I'm one of the few who gets a do-over on that front. But given how formative it was, most people remember their first and only puberty and so we get to share stories and crack jokes and everyone has a good time.

There are a few aspects of my transition, though, that are fairly unique, such as the experience of looking at a photo that was ostensibly me and seeing someone who for all intents and purposes has passed from this mortal realm.

The thing is, though, that's me! That's me there on the left! I remember exactly where I was when that photo was taken, who I was with, what I was doing, blah, blah, blah. Yet that person was a husband, a father, a brother, and a son. That person had a sperm count, a hairy chest, and some nasty BO when he got sweaty.

But me? My sweat is as pure as a mountain stream. I can exercise in the morning, literally stay in my workout clothes ALL DAY, and debate whether or not I need to take a shower before going to bed because I still smell like a floral bouquet when night falls. Also, washing my hair once a week? A dream!

I still don't really understand the concept behind dry shampoo, though. Feels like a marketing ploy of some kind. How can it be shampoo if it doesn't have any bubbles? Bar soap, liquid soap, foaming soap, dish soap: they all have bubbles. Shampoo has bubbles. Dry shampoo? That's a nope for me.

Back to the dead guy there on the left.

As fascinating as it is for me to have lived a very full life existing in the world as one gender and then getting the opportunity to live a very full life as the gender I was supposed to be from the get-go, I very much hope that I am one of the last people who have this experience. It is what it is and I am making the best of it, but all things being equal, the sooner one is able to live openly and freely as themself, the better.

I look at kids who are growing up free of so many of the restrictions that I struggled against and I marvel at the openness with which they live. Anyone who is younger than thirty is a kid to me, so I'm talking about a lot of people here. I know parents who are raising trans children and my mind explodes with joy at the idea of someone like me growing up knowing nothing but unconditional love from the most important people in their lives.

While I'm kind of crushing it and just beginning to grow into my powers, I do hope that I end up being the exception and not the norm when it comes to how trans people emerge into the world. Mostly because I just want people to live their truth as authentically as they can. But there is a little part of me that doesn't want the competition for the best book ever written on being trans.

So, if you are a parent of a really smart child who is very creative and articulate and you think they might be trans: EMBRACE THAT SHIT!

S3E16 | Cassandra At The Crossroads

First and foremost, my Insta is my diary of my transition. I have had the good fortune to share many moments of Joy, but I feel that I can't be true to my experience if I keep the Struggle in the shadows. For me, this picture captures that tension in a way that is deeply meaningful. It's my new favorite, by far.

I see a diva weighing the cost of what it took to shine this brightly. I see the weight of a past that can't be memory-wiped taking its toll. I see concern over how much time is left on the clock. I see poise and confidence competing for real estate with insecurity and fear.

I see someone who believes she will never be loved again, who is beginning to accept that she will spend the rest of her life alone. I see someone who could have sex with a different person every night but couldn't fall asleep next to any of them. Someone for whom casual holds no interest but for whom commitment is off limits.

I see a woman who is relentlessly told that she is an inspiration but is struggling to understand to what end. Who cares deeply about authenticity and thirsts for it in a culture that rewards shallow validation. Who actively participates in that culture while trying to change it.

I see someone with incredible privilege who will perpetually be at a disadvantage. Someone who did this for herself and is only beginning to appreciate the cost to others. Someone who feels guilty for choosing herself, who questions whether she is as kind and caring as she thinks she is.

I see someone just beginning to discover her powers right at the moment when they are starting to slip away. Someone who is working her issues out in full view, showing her homework in a pageant of narcissism and vulnerability.

I see someone who has proudly and without shame shared many moments of Joy. I also see someone for whom the Struggle is real. I see a middle-aged woman at the Crossroads of her life.

*#keepingitreal #deardiary #middleage
#crossroads #selflove #selfdoubt
#portraitofalady #mirrormirror*

I dare say, the decisions that I made around this time, taken together, are probably the most consequential I have made since deciding to start hormones. I was at an absolute Crossroads Moment and the options I was considering could not have been more diverse. There were three, all of which represented very different pathways that would have taken me in very different directions.

I chose wisely, and what you will see unfold over the course of Season Four is the direct result of that choice.

One of these days I will talk about what those other two options were. Lemme first see how this all plays out, though, to include the part about getting elected.

SEASON FOUR

GRACEFUL CHANGE

"What do you allow yourself?"

Those were the most powerful words I had ever heard when my therapist posed them three years ago. I was just beginning to accept that I was trans but still assumed there was nothing I could do about it.

This smile is my answer to her question. This is what I allow myself: the freedom to stop pretending to be someone I'm not and to let the person I am enjoy her time in the sun before it sets. The legs are a nice little bonus.

#transition #smile #legsfordays
#belight #findyourpath #belove

Around the time this photo was taken I spent a couple hours chatting with someone I met at that Lululemon celebration of women's empowerment held at the Kennedy Center. I told her more of my story, more of the effort to try and rapidly catch up on several decades' worth of lost experiences. I talked about how frustrating it was to have people perceive me as a well put-together, quite confident middle-aged hottie in her prime but to feel on the inside that I was still so inexperienced.

I talked about all the things that I had navigated over the past year: adjusting to radical changes in my body, to include budding breasts that society still has a complicated relationship with; figuring out all the seemingly-infinite varieties of presentation from make-up to hair to clothes to nails to literally every element that has the potential to be a canvas for your inner sense of self; learning how to manage the commodification of my body as a sexualized object that others desired, whether I wanted that or not; and when I did want it, identifying, establishing, and enforcing brand new boundaries. And as a meta experience, navigating variations in everything that I just mentioned throughout different stages of life, from teenager to young adult, on through middle age and the cusp of Senior Discount eligibility.

I ran through all of this with the woman I was talking to and she said something that, for lack of a better term, totally blew my mind: "Do you have any idea how lucky you are to have learned the lessons that every woman spends decades struggling with over the course of about a year?"

Hearing this helped me understand that I am exactly where I need to be. That I had done the work, studied and learned as intensively as I possibly could, and had made up tremendous amounts of lost ground. I began to appreciate that I was centered and grounded in the exact place where any woman my age would find herself.

That was a good day.

The only time I have ever contemplated what my life could have been like if I had transitioned earlier was when I crossed paths earlier this year with an utterly lovely young trans woman on Instagram who is about half my age. It feels presumptuous to compare myself to her—or to anyone, really—so I won't, but I will say that she is the only person I have ever met who I looked at and thought, "Yeah, that could have been my path." Not with longing or jealousy or envy—if you can't tell by now, I am rather delighted at how things are working out—but with an appreciation and admiration for someone blossoming at a much earlier stage of their life.

I'm the kind of person that tends to mourn things that have yet to happen. Like, I'm losing lots of sleep worrying that we won't have elections anymore and I won't get my press conference to discuss my opponent's use of "Bubble Bath Bikini" to try and discredit my candidacy. Those are the kinds of things I worry about, as I have control over all the witty things I'm going to say in response. But stuff that happened in the past? Remorse if it is something I did and should learn from, but not regret if it is something I objectively had no control over.

And I had no control over not transitioning earlier. Because of the lack of awareness in society about the trans identity, beginning this process even a day earlier than when I started it simply wasn't a possibility. In my particular example, it took the critical mass of a growing understanding among the medical and psychiatric communities, the platform that social media has given people to share their stories with the world, the courage and example of the first mainstream representatives of transness, and the sum total of my life experience to finally interact in a way that allowed me to take those very first steps.

To bring this full circle to the original post, the key that unlocked this door for me was hearing those words from my therapist: what do you allow yourself?

I had never asked myself that question before. The only question I knew how to ask was: "What should I do?" That "should" symbolized every learned behavior, every overcompensation, every societal role that I embraced in an effort to make sense of something I had struggled to understand my entire life: myself.

As you are reading this, if you feel like you are at a juncture in your own life where a confluence of factors has come together presenting a door, on the other side of which is a journey you are finally ready to take, maybe ask that question—what do you allow yourself?—and see what kind of an answer you come up with.

Generally speaking, I'm rarely moved by the "Pretty Picture + Inspirational Quote" genre of Instagram post, but I saw something on Pure Barre the other day that honestly rocked my world.

In a post about negative self-thought there was this line: "If someone was saying these things directly to you, would you tell them to stop?"

My dysphoria and dysmorphia lead me to say all kinds of things about myself that if anyone else—and I mean ANYONE— said to me I would shut that nonsense down in a heartbeat. Nobody gets to tell me that my body is misshapen. That I'm not feminine enough. Hell, just try and tell me to smile more and see how that goes.

So what makes me special? Why am I allowed to say negative things to myself but others can't? I spent a lot of time reflecting on that and it has helped SO MUCH in seeing those negative thoughts for what they are: groundless self-sabotage.

Enough! Enough self-doubt. Enough crying in front of the mirror. Enough insecurity about going to the freaking pool like it's a Miss Universe competition. Enough telling myself things I would NEVER let anyone else tell me. I've started telling myself the same kinds of things that many of you tell me all the time and it's making a big difference.

If you are plagued by self-critical thoughts, I ask you to think about that question: how would you react if someone else said what you are thinking?

#mirrormirroronthewall

#selflovejourney #shadowboxing

#itgetsbetter #trusttheprocess

About three and a half years ago I participated in a seminar for Change Management specialists. If you think that is ironic, just watch the season unfold. Anyway, as a Warm-Up exercise we were given a box of colored markers and asked to draw a picture that best represents how we see our role with our clients.

I drew a mirror with a question mark in the middle of it. I used the markers to make the question mark a rainbow.

Now, on the level of how I engage with my clients, my intent with this image was pretty clear: look into the mirror and see the spectrum of possibility that awaits.

I wasn't really thinking at the time about the secondary meaning behind this image: I am a queer enigma who has yet to take a discernible shape. I pieced that one together a couple months later.

I take the role of mirror as seriously with my art as I do with my work. Yes, that photo of me with the Bubble Bath Bikini? That's my art. Just watch, one day Sotheby's will be auctioning that shit for a couple million.

Anyway, with the content that I put on Instagram, I just put it out there and let people filter it through the prism of their person in whatever way that happens.

Reactions cover a fairly wide spectrum from "This is incredibly inspiring, thank you for helping me see what is possible on the other side of fear" to "you disgust me." In between there is quite a lot of territory, but for the most part, the scales lean very heavily in the direction of "thank you for sharing."

As a rule, I think that if you are a being of light and you see someone expressing their own self-love, then it is natural to see in them something worth celebrating. Conversely, if you hate yourself and see someone radiating self-love, well... I just know from personal experience that some people hate what they see in the mirror so much that they try and break it.

Do your best not to let your prism be your prison.

Thank you to everyone who offered up a question: I got tons! About my transition and my secret project, about my genitals and relationship status. Enjoy!

IF WOMENS CLOTHES WERE LIKE THE OUTFITS OF 1970s MAO'S CHINA WOULD YOU STILL TRANSITION?

Absolutely! And I'd look hot AF in them. I transitioned out of an existential need to be myself. The whole fashion, beauty culture, show my thing has honestly been a completely unexpected bonus. A welcome bonus, but never part of the plan. The plan was to save my life.

DESCRIBE YOURSELF IN ONE WORD

Intense

I'M CURIOUS ABOUT THE IDEAS BEHIND YOUR TATTOOS

Happy to share! Upper left arm are coordinates of where my three children were born and three other places that hold deep personal meaning.

The arrow shooting through infinity on my left forearm represents my goal of always moving forward.

The flower on my right forearm is me! Purple, blossoming, and looks too good to be true. But it's real.

And the butterfly is the story of my rebirth. It is built over my very first tattoo, which was a tribal Superman design that represented peak overcompensation. I rather like that I can still see the outline: it's a useful reminder that I can't erase my past, but I can move forward from it.

HOW DO YOU DEAL WITH DYSPHORIA WHEN IT GETS OVERWHELMING?

Generally speaking, I feel blessed with F**K You Confidence and a proud embrace of my trans identity that folds dysphoria into my day-to-day existence. I just assume everyone knows I'm a trans woman. A witty, fun, sexy trans woman who believes that everyone who sees her will have a better day because they saw an out and proud trans woman doing her thing.

But the dysphoria is always there. Always. Dysphoria is trauma and I don't believe that trauma ever really goes away: it can only be managed. Most days I manage it pretty well, but when I don't, when it becomes overwhelming, then I sob in front of the mirror, twisting myself in various angles to try and bring myself back into focus. Then I cry some more.

DO YOU HAVE WEINER?

Great question!

But before I answer it, I'd like to say something to all you guys who truly don't care what is down there, who send me compliments and pictures of flowers and marriage proposals: thank you! I genuinely appreciate your appreciation!

You are setting a great example for other men to follow, the ones who care SO MUCH about what is in someone's pants that they feel compelled to show everyone what is in theirs. YOU guys are the future. I believe in you.

THAT SAID, I've been very open about the fact that this girl needs her vajayjay properly installed. I've known my entire life that I need an Innie instead of an Outie and much like the next Fast and Furious movie Operation Pussycat has been pushed to Spring 2021 due to COVID.

ARE YOU SINGLE?

Right now I'm pretty much on ice. I dated a bunch of people earlier this #summeroflove and while it's great that guys accept me for who I am, mama has needs and they can't really be fulfilled with this stupid little that makes no sense to me.

Fun fact: most of my non-trans girlfriends assume that the guys who want to date me are gay.

HAHAHAHAHAHAHAHA THATS A GOOD ONE, LADIES!

The guys who are attracted to me are straight AF. In fact, ladies, show your husband or boyfriend some of my Insta pics and see how he reacts.

EXACTLY MY POINT!

But since guys are into me but can't really get into me—GET IT?—it's a frustrating situation that doesn't seem worth my time.

When I get all frisky my brain SCREAMS for something to go in, and since I'm not really a Door Number Two girl, it's not the most fulfilling of experiences.

Sex aside, I also don't have the energy for handholding and long walks in the park and stuff like that right now. I've got an empire of love to build and that is taking a lot of my energy these days.

#secretproject #keepingitreal

#youaskedforit #whysoserious

#thisiswhattranslookslike

When it comes to various projects or goals, I am not an "OMG Beyoncé just dropped a surprise album!!!" kind of girl. I set intentions for myself, but I also share them with others very openly as a means of holding myself accountable so that I actually follow through. It's one thing to think about transitioning, another to send an email to my colleagues that I am going to transition and that they should expect updated guidance on my name and bathroom usage. The same thing is going on here with this "secret project" tease mentioned at the beginning of this post.

The decisions I made during that Crossroads Moment referenced in S3E16 were beginning to bear fruit and I was feeling confident enough that they were going to happen that I could start building a little bit of hype. However, while I was more confident than I had been before, I still wasn't fully confident.

While all the work of scoping and planning and plotting this project was going on behind the scenes (in other words, off of Instagram) I was dropping little hints in my posts. Hashtags and references that some people paid attention to, others completely missed or didn't care about. I knew they were there, though, and they served as additional logs on the fire I had lit under my own ass to make progress on this project.

I would love to rewrite history a bit and say that's what the photo in the post represents, but sadly I'm not THAT intentional. But it is a good line, so I'll leave it in.

Hi! I'm Cassandra Grace, President and CEO of Graceful Change LLC. I would love to hear your feedback on options for my company's logo.

This is the #secretproject that I have been mercilessly teasing for some time: I've started a company, the purpose of which is to help the world help itself.

The basic idea is a full-service consultancy and media platform to help others—individuals and organizations, companies and governments—develop their potential and purpose. I've been working in the Change Management field for many years and more recently I've been managing a fair amount of change myself. Speaking of which...

Make no mistake, my trans identity is the beating heart of this company, an unmistakable Proof of Concept of the power of evolutionary change. I've been working with investors, a marketing team, and very well-placed advisors, all of whom believe in this out and proud trans woman's vision.

That vision is to become a globally recognized brand that transforms the way change is managed. And become Oprah's trans Bestie. #priorities .

Before I do that, though, I need to settle on a logo and I'd like your help! I've been working with the ridiculously talented @nicoleshyti on the branding and upcoming website and I would love to hear reactions to these concepts. These are not final designs—and for those wondering, the color palette we are working with is basically what I am wearing!—so your feedback is truly welcome and appreciated!

I look forward to sharing so much more in the coming weeks and months. Thank you to everyone for your support and encouragement! It has given me tremendous strength and fueled my faith in this effort. More than most of you know. Thank you.

#ifyoubuildit #bossladymindset
#transpride #justgettingstarted
#womanownedbusiness

I invite you to visit my company's website...

www.gracefulchange.me

A massive Thank You to my friends at Roman USA for gifting me this outfit—earrings included!!—to help build out my #bosslady wardrobe. I spent much of Sunday trying on pretty much everything in the store and there are a few more pieces that I'll be highlighting in the coming weeks.

This outfit, though, represents the energy and confidence that I'm bringing to my business. I'm humbled that everyone at Roman USA believes in what I am doing and very grateful to them for their support.

Thanks again to everyone for YOUR support and please accept my apologies for not being as active in commenting as I'd like.

#womensupportingwomen

#femaleentrepreneur #transvisibility

#womensupportingwomeninbusiness

Not too long ago I was interviewed for a profile in Washington Technology magazine about my company, Graceful Change. The original draft introduced me in the following way: "While Ms. Grace was working on her career transition she was going through a very personal and physical transition, from being a man to becoming a woman."

I know that the author had every best intention and I know that this is how my transition looks to most people, so the phrasing is understandable. My reality, however, is a little more complicated. We chatted a bit and here is how the sentence appeared as published: "While Ms. Grace was working on her career transition she was going through a very personal and physical transition, having finally embraced her transgender identity."

That is an important distinction. I was never a man and I am not now becoming a woman. I did, however, exist in the world for quite a long time as a man and I am only now learning what it is like to exist in the world as a woman. One constant throughout all of this, though, is that I have always been trans.

It took me some time to get to the point where I really understood what that means and founding this business was an integral part of this process. By grounding my company in my personal application of Change Management principles, by leading with my transness as the core value proposition I offer, I found myself healthily embracing the totality of my life's experience.

When I commit to something, I commit, and I embraced my transition with hungry wonder. The wide-eyed "Girl Meets World" vibe of the similarly-titled Season One earlier in this book? I reveled in the pure, innocent delight of finally experiencing the adolescence I was always meant to have. It was a burst of rainbow confection into my veins that brought me incredible relief and an explosion of unabashed discovery which you saw in "Countdown to V-Day."

Drunk with freedom, I pushed my expression of femininity so far beyond the limits of anything I could ever have imagined. And then I pushed further. How far could I go? Where was the line? Was there a line? I hope you enjoyed "Quarantine Qrazy" as much as I and a core group of very devoted Gentleman Admirers among my Instagram followers clearly did.

But enough is enough. It's time to settle down. I look back at these first three "seasons" and I see rapid growth, an almost desperate "making up for lost time" energy at play. I see the girl, I see the adolescent, I see the young, adventurous, maybe even reckless woman. That pace of change couldn't continue and I am so relieved that it didn't.

I look at this photo and I see a reflection of this synthesis of experiences. I see an acceptance that I existed in the world for so long as a man and a comfort with having finally earned the relief of existing in the world as a woman. I see someone wearing pants and a button-up shirt and not giving a damn about what those items of clothing may represent in a gendered sense. I see Next-Level confidence and an awareness that I am right where I need to be at this point in my life.

For those who saw my Story yesterday, I had Breast Augmentation surgery. For those who didn't see my Story, YOU HAVE NO IDEA THE GOLDEN CONTENT YOU ARE MISSING!

Anyway, they are a little hard to see because of all the camouflage I am wearing, but I am beyond thrilled with how everything feels. Honestly, I'm very pleasantly surprised at the sense of peace and calm and confidence that I already feel.

Yes, I feel more confident. I know.

Even this T-shirt... I got this a few weeks ago at Target but didn't feel comfortable wearing it. Until now.

My style is generally high femme, but I know that my face is very androgynous a la Tilda Swinton/David Bowie love child. So I've expressed my inner diva with a rather femme-leaning wardrobe. Until recently. I'm starting to get comfortable wearing pants again. Wearing a button up shirt. I might even consider trying to rock a blazer.

Between starting my business and getting BA, though, I'm finding—to my surprise and delight—that I'm getting more IDGAF self-confidence in my presentation. Which is also coming as a huge relief as it allows me to focus more on my inner self and not my outward appearance.

Many thanks to everyone who has reached out and wished me well. I'm off painkillers and feeling pretty swell. Or swollen, as the case may be. Tomorrow morning I get to shower and see what the girls actually look like underneath all this wrapping.

#wontyoubemyneighbor

And then I got top surgery.

Not too long ago, my Bestie said the following about my boobs: "The best thing about you getting boobs is that you no longer talk about boobs."

I don't know what your impression is of the boob content up to this point, but let me tell you, whatever I have included in this book is but a fraction of the attention that I devoted to my boobs on my Instagram. From photos to comments to Ben and Jerry's updates on my Story: much of my Instagram up to this point was Boob Talk.

Now that some time has passed since the surgery, I would have to say that my Bestie has a solid point. The absolute bar-none biggest surprise of getting top surgery is that they feel like they have always been there. There is no "OMG GUYS LOOK AT MY BEWBS CAN YOU BELIEVE IT I HAVE BEWBS?!?!" None of it.

Instead, there is, "Ugh, I really should have worn that sports bra to barre class" and that's it. Do I have fun with cleavage in my photos? Yes. Do I enjoy the heft and the curve and the awareness that they are part of my body? Yes. Do I frequently play "Bulletproof Soul" and "Cherish the Day" on a loop at the end of the day and put on a show in my living room while finishing whatever bottle of red needs some attention? No!

"Frequently" implies some level of irregularity. I do that shit every night and it is a glorious tradition. It also probably explains why all my neighbors put their blinds down, but whatever.

One other thing. For those of you who know what an "unboxing video" is, let's just say that I did one for the Gram and it was a one-take wonder.

I wonder what left those marks?

Ten months.

Ten months of living openly as myself, of stepping into situation after situation with the blind confidence of self-love.

Ten months of experimenting with makeup and skincare and diet and exercise regimens; of nothing but estrogen running through my veins.

Ten months of posting picture after picture of my evolving relationship with my body, of experimentation with fashion and growing confidence in my presentation.

Ten months ago I was living a dream I never thought possible. Ten months later....I'm living a dream I never thought possible. But the dream looks and feels so different in so many ways I just didn't anticipate or plan for.

Much like gender itself, I've come to appreciate that my transition is not a binary. It had a beginning but it really has no end, that it will continue for the rest of my life. So, like, at least another hundred years.

And much like the past ten months have felt like a decade given the intensity of this experience, I expect those hundred to feel like a thousand. In the best possible way.

#justgettingstarted #thegiftoflife
#transitiontuesday #makeuponpoint

A couple months into openly presenting as female, so summer 2019, I was chatting with a friend I have known for a very long time. We hadn't seen each other in years, and this was the first time she was seeing Cassandra. I was giddy with the euphoria of being able to express myself openly and to feed my vanity a little further I asked her what she thought about my whole deal.

Without missing a beat, she said: "It's still you, you just seem so much happier."

I was devastated. Forget about all the effort that I had put into my outfit—and yes, let's please forget about it because I am sure it was not as fabulous as I thought—I felt like my entire reason for transitioning had been invalidated. I felt like she was totally missing the point, refusing to see all the effort that I had put into leaving "him" behind and embracing the "her" that had been trapped inside for so long.

With time, though, I came to understand the wisdom of her observation. While I have left "him" behind, this entire process has been about embracing me, the me who has always been there and found various ways of expressing herself, but also struggled mightily with incredible amounts of mind/body tension.

These two photos side by side do a really good job of underscoring the moment of "being" that I am finally enjoying after so much time and effort spent "becoming." Early in my transition, all my metrics of visible change were grounded in a sliding scale with "M" on one side and "F" on the other. Many of the "Then and Now" photographic comparisons that I have shared here reflect movement along that spectrum. This one is a little different.

While I still see elements of "him" over there on the left—I'm not blind—I don't look at the photo on the right and see more of a woman. In other words, I don't look at these two photos and think "him" vs. "her." Instead, I just see degrees of me.

I look at the photo on the left and I see someone fully in the throes of the "OMG CAN YOU BELIEVE THIS IS FINALLY HAPPENING?!?!" phase of her second adolescence. I see someone radiating so much euphoria that she doesn't fully appreciate that she's not pulling it off as well as she thinks she is. I also see someone who doesn't care whether she is pulling it off, someone who is exploding with the blind confidence of newfound freedom. And I see someone trying really hard with all that highlighter and pink eye shadow to make sure everyone knows what's what.

I look at the photo on the right and I see someone who is more comfortable in her skin, who has found her look, her groove. I see someone wearing that dress with the calm confidence of having earned it, who doesn't need to send any signals to reassure herself—or anyone else—that this is indeed happening. I see someone having effortless fun with her hair and bringing casual elegance to her eye makeup game. I see someone who exudes "I got this" cool energy.

A few weeks ago my therapist told me: "You know, Cassandra, you are so self-absorbed, I'm not sure you are capable of being in a relationship with anyone other than yourself."

She meant it as a Good Thing, a healthy development as I leave behind the last echoes of insecurity from the Before Times. And I think she is right.

I stopped dating earlier this summer for a number of reasons, one of which is that it just got boring. Yes, yes, sex is there for the taking, but it really doesn't interest me without some kind of emotional connection. And I don't think I'm capable of that any more.

This isn't a sob story! I'm good, truly. I also had a couple of Trulys while taking these pics, but I digress.

I have to say, it's weird to have come to this point but it kind of feels right. I'm trying to spread out the love that I otherwise would devote to a relationship in a less intense way to my friends, and I'm also channeling a lot of it into my business. #everybodywins.

And for anyone wondering, bottom surgery is "merely" so that I can look in the mirror and see what I've known for my entire life needs to be there. Period.

Well, without the period. Lucky me.

I never get tired of that joke.

#girlsdayout #selflove #memyselfandi

One of the more unexpected developments of this past year is having my girlfriends look at some of these "Then and Now" photos that I post and tell me how attractive they found that guy on the left. Moreover, I have had some straight-up say that they would have pursued him like a heat-seeking missile.

This bothers me for several reasons.

First of all, for the most part, I just don't find him attractive. I didn't at the time and I don't now. That androgynous period when I was going through my "Trans Who Fell To Earth" phase that we got a glimpse of in S3E8? Totally. But prior to that? I just don't get it.

The "sad little man-boy who is lost and will do anything in exchange for meaning and purpose" vibe just doesn't...wait a minute...hold on... Ok, ok, I think I get the nature of the appeal.

Beyond the aesthetics of it all, though, hearing my girlfriends talk about how attractive they found the beta version of me is just weird AF. Every freaking time I post a photo of "him" as part of these Transition Tuesday posts, invariably one of my girlfriends says something about how hot they found him and how they would have "hunted him down" or "pushed people out of the way" to get at him. Every single freaking time.

I mean, I appreciate the validation of my identity that my girlfriends talking about him as someone else signifies, but still... that was me!!! The sassy girl you swap "OMG OBSESSED WITH YOUR LOOK" with is very confused by all the attention "he" is getting. From what I know and have experienced so far, Brunch Besties don't talk about how much they want to finger-bang each other over mimosas, so it really does bother me when my girlfriends sexualize "him" the way they do.

Question: Do I need to find different Brunch Besties?

Anyway, aside from the poor taste in men my girlfriends have and the weirdness of them lusting after someone who is fundamentally me, another reason I don't like hearing this is because it reminds me what it was like to fall asleep next to another human being. To wake up next to them. To celebrate holidays and mark anniversaries together. All of those events and experiences are things that I still remember, many of which I have quite fond memories of. Being told how desirable I was as a partner then just serves as a reminder of how undesirable I am as a partner now.

Sex? I'm not talking about sex. Sex is everywhere, sex is easy. It's like tennis, right? Find someone who is as bad at it as you are and it's still a lot of fun. And unlike tennis, there are still lots of people who are into sex. But relationships? Not so much.

Let's break it down when it comes to my age bracket.

A man pushing fifty? Whatever the motivation on the partner side, if that dude wants company, he is going to have it. Regardless of orientation, there are no shortage of options available across a wide range of age.

A woman pushing fifty, well...that's a different story, isn't it? Eat, Pray, and get used to learning how to Love yourself. Find someone in a similar situation, though, and there are countless vineyards for the two of you to enjoy.

A trans woman pushing fifty? Lemme just say that I think I'm going to have lots of time to myself to write a few more books.

GRACEFUL CHANGE

I'm overjoyed to reveal the final logo for my company! It is presented here in the three variations we will use depending on format and need.

Many thanks to the incredibly talented (and very patient!) @nicoleshyti for her inspired work and for everyone here who offered their feedback on the preliminary designs.

This design seemed to click with people on a deeper, visceral level and I think it best represents the power of infinite growth that is the foundation of my brand.

Much love and appreciation to everyone for their support and encouragement! In particular, thank you to Roman USA for their gift of these pants to help build out my stylish #bossbabe wardrobe.

I look forward to sharing more news as Graceful Change LLC continues to evolve.

#alwaysmovingforward

#womanownedbusiness #femaleentrepreneur

#thisiswhattranslookslike #transvisibility

While Instagram remains my primary online platform, the website for my company has a blog called "The Garden." Here is one of the first articles that I wrote for it, a little something that lays out my thinking on why I started this company and what I offer as a Change Management specialist who happens to be trans.

Mars and Venus and the Cosmic Space In Between
(The Whole Trans Thing)

In some people's minds, a trans individual is by default someone who needs help, not someone who could possibly offer it to others. I'm not saying YOU are that person, but let's be honest, that perception is still out there. Not only am I exceedingly proud of being trans, but I happen to think that it allows me to help others in ways that I simply couldn't prior to transitioning.

Intrigued? Please read on...

Obviously there are exceptions to every rule, but Type A "Excuse My Behavior Because of How Much of a Genius I Am" Disruptors tend to be from Mars, and authorities on "How Embracing Vulnerability Can Empower You to Unleash Your Inner Boss Lady Goddess" often hail from Venus. While that is a rather simplistic binary, it's not difficult to think of examples who fit neatly into either end of that spectrum.

Both of those approaches are quite popular, and I am in no way trying to knock them. What makes my approach a little different, though, is that I come neither from Mars, nor from Venus, but from the vast cosmic space in between. Of course, there are many friendly, empathetic, vulnerable men, as well as lots of strong, authoritative "don't

eff with me" women. No question! My transness, though, has empowered me with an exceedingly rare mélange of experiences and perspectives that allows for connections across a multitude of divides.

I am sharing all of this because it is core to the values of my company and to the methodology that I use. That's the glass half full interpretation. Another way of looking at it is that I just offended 98% of the population. Yikes! In all seriousness, my trans identity is fundamental to who I am and the unique value that I offer. My aim in addressing it here in some detail is to help you better understand what a strength it represents and how it helps me help you.

Traditionally speaking, many of the dominant narratives related to the trans identity still tend to focus on what is between someone's legs rather than what is between their ears. Furthermore, when defined by outsiders to this experience, these narratives often fall into two distinct categories: The Spectacle of Otherness or The Path to Assimilation.

My transition narrative is neither of these.

It is a story of transcendence not just of gender, but also of expectations and privilege, of assumptions and fear, of overcoming learned behaviors that limit. It is a story of living joyfully and purposefully through embracing my identity and in so doing, unleashing the potential that had always been there, just buried under layers and layers of fear. This is the part of the story that anyone who I connect with understands on a visceral level.

For me personally, this is the element of being trans that I find magical. I take great pride and satisfaction in being able to turn something that is still too-commonly viewed as "other" into something accessible and relatable. There is an existential alchemy to that process that I am honored to be a part of whenever it happens.

As I share my story of embracing authenticity and living with purpose, many people ask themselves: "Is this the job I want to do?" "Is this relationship right for me?" "Why am I doing (fill in the blank with something harmful) to my body?" In a professional context, the unavoidably positive energy of my transness serves as a powerful conversation-starter that helps me act as a better catalyst for organizational change. We can all hopefully agree that groups function better when inhibitions are removed, lines of communication are pure, and fear is taken out of the equation. These are lessons that are powerfully reinforced by the explicit example of living the truth that my trans identity represents.

I want to be clear that everything I share here in The Garden I share from my perspective and mine alone. This is especially true when it comes to why I think my experience as a trans woman helps me excel at what I do professionally. I talk about my experience solely in the context of MY experience. While I care deeply about seeing the trans community thrive, I am not speaking for anyone else's experience here but mine.

One other thing worth noting: trans people have been around forever. It's not like there was some mass infestation of radioactive genderqueer spiders a couple of years ago and then all of a sudden *Pose* is racking up Emmy nominations. In fact, in several cultures, trans individuals had been sought out for their perspective because they were trans. They were shamans, mystical leaders who were revered—not ridiculed—because of their "otherness."

To paraphrase the great Justin Timberlake, I am part of bringing sexy back to the idea of the trans identity as a unique perspective to be sought out. I aim to be a voice that is listened to because of the value of my transness, not shunned because of the perceived flaws in it. Not just listened to, though, but hired to run your company's next team-building offsite or help you navigate that personal crossroads that you are stuck on.

Come on, I'm running a business here!

And since I am running a business, if you found the above compelling, please check out www.gracefulchange.me/services for a description of all the ways I can help you.

Air Date: August 29, 2020

My breasts are the subject of a harassment investigation. Intrigued? Let me tell you a tale...

In early March I went for my Breast Augmentation consultation. My surgeon recommended that I put panty hose socks filled with dry quinoa equal to the size of the implants I was considering into my bra. Done. I went to work the next day and the sensation was magical. I walked around like I was floating on air, even though I had a pound of quinoa in my bra.

A work acquaintance—a woman I had taken to Barre class as my "friend" earlier in the year—came to talk to me about something and during our chat I asked if she noticed anything different. She said no, and I did that whole "eyes down here" thing and explained everything I just told you: that I had a BA consultation the day before and was walking around with quinoa in my bra.

She said: "I guess it looks nice," and that was that.

Or so I thought.

Fast forward to last month and I find out that I am the subject of a harassment investigation that she initiated. Alongside my solicitation to examine my breasts, the content of my Instagram has been cited as potential grounds for harassment. Specifically, my participation in the pillow challenge and my Bubble Bath Bikini picture. Why? Because these were posts that I mentioned to her WHILE WE WERE AT HOME TEXTING ABOUT WORK AND OUR KIDS DURING THE PANDEMIC AND SHE ASKED ME WHAT I WAS UP TO.

I swear to sweet baby Jesus that my first reaction when I was informed of this last month was uncontrollable laughter. Just being honest. I said something like "Do you realize what a landmark day this is for trans rights?! You are investigating my boobs and I haven't even had top surgery yet! I feel so validated!!!"

Yeah, that's how I roll. The sassy bish you engage with here on Instagram? That's me. 24/7.

With the passage of time, however, my delight at this incident has waned. I've given a deposition, submitted text histories, had character witnesses interviewed. I also learned that the decision to open this investigation was supported by a fair number of people.

Additionally, this is the entire story. Nothing else happened. Other than the whole "me being trans" thing and someone perceiving my celebration of my body as a threat to theirs.

That this happened because I am trans is a no-brainer. But it's not an automatic no-brainer to fight back. I need to weigh the Greater Good and the impact of all of the attention that me pursuing a discrimination claim will bring. I have enough attention to deal with as it is. There are enough incidents of far greater harm being done that need to be adjudicated.

I'm talking to people about what to do, gathering perspectives from the LGBTQ+ community, and I intend to do what makes the most sense for the community, not what might make me feel good in the moment.

As silly as this all seems, though, it's not. There are some pretty substantial issues concerning the validity of my body as feminine, the acceptance and acknowledgment of trans women as equals to other women, the relevance of social media activity to the workplace, blah, blah, blah. Serious stuff.

And I am taking it very seriously, to include weighing whether I need to take a principled stance or whether the smart and also right thing to do is just to roll with this, not bring even more attention to my boobs, and accept that in the Grand Pantheon of Bad Things that happen to trans people, this is a f**king nothingburger.

I should find out in the next couple weeks whether my pre-BA boobs are guilty of harassment. God only knows what they could be charged with now...

And just when you thought there wouldn't be any more boob content!

To be continued...

Air Date: September 16, 2020

The verdict on my boobs is in: NOT GUILTY!!!

Recently I shared that I have been the subject of a harassment investigation at work. Details are in a post where I am showing my boobs. No, not that one. The other one. No! Not that post, the other one!

Anyway, before I go any further, I want to say a massive thank you to everyone who contributed their thoughts and support. The discussion we had was immeasurably helpful to me and I appreciate everyone who offered their perspective.

As far as the results of the months-long investigation, I could not have hoped for a better outcome. I was impressed with the professionalism, with the respect for my identity, and for the clear communication to me that people involved in this process have learned a little bit as it unfolded.

That said, the anxiety, uncertainty, and overall stress that I've felt has had a major impact on me. But this impact has not been entirely negative.

Well ahead of today's outcome, I came to appreciate this entire experience as a valuable lesson. In objectification of my body. In acceptance and tolerance, or lack thereof, of trans bodies as valid. But after today, also in how far we have come. It is definitely a step in the right direction.

I am now going to step in the direction of a wine-fueled bubble bath and I will not be taking any pictures.

Probably not.

Maybe just a few.

#celebrategoodtimes #humpday
#indeed #transwomenarewomen
#girlslikeus #wontbeerased

As a trans woman, the Venn Diagram of "trans" and "woman" looks a lot like my boobs when I smoosh them together: there is a lot of overlap, but there are still some things that fall clearly into their own distinct spaces.

There are specific biological experiences that I am never going to have. While I know that there are some people who insist that this invalidates my existence as a woman, I would say the following to them: nobody asks me when my last period was when they call me "ma'am."

Just saying.

On the other hand, there are specific biological experiences that are pretty unique to being trans. Researching "foot reduction surgery" for example, is a bit of a niche thing that most non-trans women probably don't spend too much time on.

When it comes to objectification and sexualization of our bodies, however, this is something that all women experience. As horrible as this might sound, being the subject of a harassment investigation that passed judgment on the validity of my body was a life lesson that I am quite grateful for.

Given my age and my privilege and when and where I began my transition, I have been insulated from a lot of the life lessons that all women go through, trans or otherwise. There are plusses and minuses to this, but it's not something I'm going to change so I just have to deal with it. I mean, it's not like I'm going to re-enroll in Middle School just to live through that shit again, this time as a girl. Thanks, but no.

Since I kind of just dove into the deep end of Cougardom tits first, a lot of my emergence into the world as a woman has been greeted with "OMG, you're so brave!" and "OMG, you're so hot!" and "OMG, you're such a good writer" and that's pretty much it. I know, I know, rough life.

That's exactly why I am so appreciative for all of this having happened. As immature as my initial reaction to hearing that I was the subject of a harassment investigation may appear—delight over the validation of my boobs that it represented—having my body and my pride in my body discussed, examined, and adjudicated was an utterly humiliating experience that I am very glad to have had.

To all the empowering women I've come to know over the past year through Lululemon: thank you for your support and your friendship! That said, you are ALL responsible for bailing me out of jail when I get arrested for public indecency because of these leggings I just got.

I tried these on the other day and was told again and again and again that they looked great.

I had some concerns, especially as I JUST emerged from a harassment claim made against my breasts. Nevertheless, I persisted in getting them and I wore them to Barre right away.

But come on! Like, for real: I can go out in public like this?! We're all cool with me basically wearing a gigantic arrow pointing in the direction of my hoohah?!?!

I mean, I know I am.

#herewegoagain #purebarre
#lululemonleggings #thesweatlife

I legit did not think that I could walk around in public showing something so pubic.

That's it. That's the reflection. I know a perfect sentence when I see it. We're good. On to the next episode.

Hello autumn, my old friend...

This Anthropologie dress means so much to me, it has come to represent so much change in my life.

It was one year ago today that I stepped onto a runway wearing this dress. Those pictures were the first ones that I put on my Instagram when I started it a few weeks later.

That moment was my debutante ball, my fashion coming out party. It was my first real brave step forward into believing that I represented something that others would want to see. I've clearly taken a giant leap since.

Toward the end of last year I posted this dress again when all of a sudden I sprouted hips. I could not believe the difference that I saw, the increased confidence and command that I had in my body.

And here we are again, this time with more confidence, more command, and a lot more going on in the Curves Department.

Thanks for letting me share these milestones with you in a safe, supportive environment. For me, Instagram is a vital oasis of support and acceptance made possible by the kindness of good people from around the world. Thank you for being a part of that.

#myanthrophoto #transwoman

#bekindalways #helloautumn

#gratitudeattitude

A s I mentioned earlier, once I found my footing on Instagram and began to take it seriously as a living diary of my transition, I knew that the content I was sharing would form the first draft of some kind of book. The idea for that book, however, was a very conventional one. You know, just lots of words on a page kind of thing. By late summer I had pulled together a fairly tight treatment and had started pitching it around. To give you a sense of where my head was at, here is the introduction to that treatment:

SHAMELESS
Conquering Fear With Grace

by Cassandra Grace

To conquer something conjures specific images: victory, defeat, perhaps violence. Doing something with grace evokes quite different feelings: compassion, forgiveness, even love. To conquer fear with grace synthesizes the hard and the soft, the traditional associations of male and female. I represent that synthesis, and my book will convey a universally relatable message that is singular in its messenger.

I have seen my story open so many eyes, crack open so many doors over the past year and a half. During this time, I have connected with thousands of people in person, hundreds of thousands online, inspiring them to look inward and rethink what is possible. This book is the cornerstone of an uplifting empire of empathy I am building with my company, Graceful Change, through which I seek to connect with millions. I do not want to change the world. I want to help the world change itself.

I believe that this begins with a book that tells the transition story in a novel way. Not a Tolstoy novel way, but in a tight 300-page romp which defies expectations of struggle and assimilation and instead highlights the transformative power of stepping fearlessly into the world with joy and authenticity. This story takes something that is still seen as a curiosity at best, a shameful deviation at worst, and flips it into a universally relatable story of the power of positive change.

A s far as the content of the book, well, like I said, the stories that I have shared on my Instagram are the stories that I intended to share in the book:

How did I go from getting an eye shadow tutorial at Sephora to being featured by them in a social media campaign seen by hundreds of thousands of people? How did buying my first top in a brick and mortar Anthropologie store lead to me walking in a runway show for them a mere seven months later? How did modeling Lululemon leggings result in being invited to the Kennedy Center for a celebration of Women's Empowerment?

The stories are enjoyable (and the pictures are great!) but the lessons of fearlessness and persistence in goal-setting, follow-through, and iteration, among many others, are widely applicable to anyone stepping into change. Or walking a runway. I have excellent tips on how to do that.

Sound familiar?

Seeing this photo and seeing it juxtaposed against a photo of me wearing the same dress a year earlier helped me understand the storytelling potential of the visual content that I have shared on my Instagram. It wasn't until I was having a strategy session about a month later with my business partner, Scott Force, however, before all the pieces clicked and the concept for the book you are currently reading was born.

It was October 2020. The website for my company was about to launch and I had recently given an interview for that feature on my approach to Change Management for Washington Technology magazine. Scott and I got together for a strategy session to talk about all these developments and to kick around ideas for how to best pitch the book proposal that I just quoted from.

Scott had been talking about the idea of self-publishing *SHAMELESS* ever since I came up with the pitch. I was skeptical for lots of reasons. I knew how much work I would have to do to write the book and I wanted a contract—up front—as an incentive. At the same time, there was no guarantee anyone would actually offer me a contract, and even if they did, given how long it takes a book to go through a traditional publisher, best case scenario it doesn't come out until late 2021 or early 2022. We both wanted the book to be a calling card for my company, a Manifesto of Change that would create some buzz and generate some business. Waiting until 2022 didn't feel like the right thing to do.

I couldn't get past the idea, though, of people dismissing my book because it was self-published. For as much as I embrace change and am bold with my fashion and showing my body and all that, I'm rather Old School when it comes to certain things, and the cachet and status of having a book deal was one of them. I wanted the respect of someone blessing my idea with a contract and I wanted a publisher to be financially vested in the success of my book so that it would do some of the heavy lifting of promoting it.

We kept on talking about this, kept on going over the same ground, and then one of those moments where persistence paid off just dropped from above.

What about a picture book? A coffee table book? What about a fashion-themed book? It all just snow-balled into reality and as we were talking, I pulled up the side-by-side of me in this dress that I had recently posted as a Transition Tuesday post. We started talking about how powerful that image is, how much of a story of change it tells on its own.

This was something I could get behind, something that I would feel good about self-publishing. I mean, it was content that I already "published" in a way, so it's not like I need anyone's blessing to put this out there for others to see. That said, I am hoping for a bidding war among traditional publishers over *Grace In Transition: The Next Four Seasons*.

Idea in hand, I left that meeting feeling excited about the book I was about to pull together, but I still had absolutely zero idea how I would go about the self-publishing piece. That's where the absolutely amazing, relentlessly fierce, endlessly entrepreneurial Christina Glickman comes into the story. I cannot talk about the behind-the-scenes of this book without talking about her.

Our paths crossed on Instagram early in 2020 and I was instantly drawn to her energy. Like, if adrenaline were anthropomorphized, it would look like Christina. When she announced the publication of her book *Xtra: The Art of Being* I immediately pre-ordered it from Amazon the day it was available. This was early in the pandemic, I was devouring every bit of connection and inspiration I could find to compensate for the social isolation, and her book was a welcome blast of insanely positive energy.

Fast forward to late October when the concept for the book you are currently loving was born. Just a few days later, Christina announced the start of a mentoring program to empower women. Of course, in this announcement I recognize the soothing, confident voice of the Universe telling me exactly what I should do. I reach out, ask about her book, and as it turns out, she self-published through Gatekeeper Press. She tells me EVERYTHING I need to know to get started, gives me every last detail about her experience, just answers every question and anticipates all the ones I didn't know I should be asking.

And now you know the rest of the story. *

*how many times do I have to mention how old I am? Yes, I am on Instagram. Yes, I speak emoji fluently. But dammit, that's a pretty big reference from when I was growing up and if you don't get it, that's why we have Google!

We've all seen the "DM US FOR COLLAB!" stuff that is part of the Instagram business model.

Yesterday I got an email from a Brand Ambassador of a "female self-love and wellness company" asking if I would be interested in repping their product. I was asked what my rates were for a post, three Stories, and a Reel.

The product? Vibrators.

Yeah, I'm not gonna lie, that made me feel pretty good. Not in the way the product is intended, but we'll get there eventually.

#goodvibrations #goodvibesonly
#comingattractions #comingsoon !!

Air Date: August 29, 2020

Becoming an Influencer is not a goal of mine, at least not in the meaning of that word in the social media sense. But getting to the point where brands see me as someone that they would want to work with, well, from a representational standpoint that has always been important to me and one of the reasons for my Instagram. I never saw something like that growing up and if I had, it would have been a factor in shaping the further course of my life.

I have it on good authority—the people who reach out to me and tell me so—that putting myself out there the way I do is a net positive for trans representation. I am very conscious of this and it is my primary motivation for doing the "Influencer" stuff. The occasional free shit is nice, though, I'm not going to lie.

Sidebar: the top and necklace in this photo were gifted from my friends at Roman as part of a modest deal I had with them. Thanks, ladies!

Do I think I deserve the Congressional Medal of Freedom for my efforts? Not yet, but if my sculpted ass got me to the Kennedy Center, I'm certainly on my way. Furthermore, Rush Limbaugh received it for being a giant dick, so if history's pendulum swings in my favor, this vibrator deal just might be my ticket.

I believe that the kind of visible representation I do furthers the acceptance of trans people into society and that is something that means a lot to me. It also means a lot to be seen as someone for whom this product could be of use. So much so, that I wrote the following email back to the company letting them down gently and keeping the door open for a possible collaboration down the road:

To: The Lovely People At ▮▮▮▮▮▮▮

From: Cassandra Grace

_____

I am being 100% honest here: there is nothing more I would love than to be able to rep your product. I would do it for free, I would do it with all my heart. It would mean so much to me.

But as a trans woman who was supposed to have had bottom surgery in April of this year, but because of COVID had her vagina slip through her fingers (I love that line), I sadly can't speak to your product with the authenticity that is so important to me.

My surgery has been rescheduled for January 2021 and I hope very much that sometime next Spring I will have the pleasure—literally—of being able to test your product. I have waited nearly half a century to finally experience the body that I should have been given at birth. Provided everything goes smoothly, there will be much celebration.

Although I have tried, there really aren't enough words to describe how happy your email made me. I have had many wonderful experiences of acceptance into sisterhood, but none quite like this. Thank you for a story that I will share with joy for the rest of my life.

— Cassandra

MAJOR ANNOUNCEMENT!

I posted this picture in my Story yesterday with the caption: "Prepping for my Canadian citizenship exam." The implication, of course, that I was wearing red and white. And that Hotness is on the exam.

Many more people than I expected asked if I was actually moving to Canada. Or if I was already there.

TO BE CLEAR: I am not moving to Canada.

In fact, not only am I staying in the US, but I would like to announce that I will be running for President no later than 2032. We already have a great slogan: "Win With Grace!"

I'm curious what my advisors think of me using this photo to announce my candidacy. Since we already made clear that CEOs wear bikinis, though, then it's about damned time that a US President wore a bra. Hopefully I won't be the first.

#whynotme #letsdothis

#imnotjoking #justwatch

#itsabouttime #winwithgrace

As far as the seriousness of my bid for the presidency, I will merely say this: I am hard-pressed to think of something that I set as an intention that I have not ultimately followed through on.

And yes, I am very aware of the assumptions I am making about the continued existence of democratic elections in this country. If those assumptions don't hold up, then don't forget about that little bit of foreshadowing all the way back in S2E13.

What I am saying is that there are multiple pathways to victory.

Also, that "CEOs wear bikinis" reference? There was a lot of swimsuit content on my Insta toward the end of the summer. Just saying for those who might be interested…

Friends! There is a link in my bio to a feature that Roman USA produced on my love for their clothes. Being featured by them is truly one of my proudest moments and I am honored to share it with you. Please let me know what you think!

This amazing jacket I'm wearing is what pulled me into their store a year ago. It's not just their clothes that I love, though. I value their friendship, their enthusiasm for all my exploits, and especially their open embrace of my trans identity.

They are an integral part of my story and I am so proud to be a part of theirs.

#transvisibility #femaleentrepreneur #womensupportingwomeninbusiness

When the lovely people at Roman asked if I wanted to be featured as one of their VIP customers, of course I said yes. My relationship with them means a lot to me and quite honestly there is no brand more represented in my closet than theirs.

I had no idea how this would turn out, though, and when I saw it, I was in shock. I wrote earlier about how I view myself as a mirror, how my job is to reflect back the best version of someone. Seeing this feature felt like a mirror was being held up for me. It helped me see how others see me, it helped me see with even more clarity the impact sharing my story has had, what my openness and visibility in putting myself out there can achieve.

I liked this feature so much that I reached out to the beyond-her-years multi-talented woman who pulled it together, Grace Venes-Escaffi, and hired her to do the design work on this book. I am very lucky to have such a creative and hard-working partner bring the vision for this book to life.

WHAT'S CASSANDRA WEARING?
A ROMAN USA CLIENT FEATURE

A little over a year ago, a tall blonde woman walked into our store for the first time. She was so curious, excited, and chatty about fashion, like a kid in a candy store! She tried on our boldest gowns and fell in love with the styles. Fast forward to today, that same woman has a closetful of ROMAN pieces, and important places to wear them! As a CEO and fashionista, she always looks her best and picks outfits that emphasize her bold personality. She has infectious positive energy, amazing confidence and is uniquely herself. We are so excited to introduce Cassandra Grace and share her feature Style Profile: "What's Cassandra Wearing?"

Describe your personal style in 3 words.

Exuberant. Creative. Authentic.

What's your favorite way to elevate daily looks?

I love coordinating my eye makeup with my outfit. Fashion is an expression of the soul and the eyes are the window into that soul. I want people to notice me for what I'm wearing and then connect with me through the sincerity and passion that I express through my eyes, so I think of my eyes as the most important accessory to whatever I am wearing.

What's a closet piece you have way too many of?

Skirts! I have a go-to handful for now, but especially when I was in my younger phase of fashion I went and bought so many skirts because I though they're so cute and girly and fun, but I definitely have upgraded and use a selection of favorites, and branched out with other pieces.

How does ROMAN fit into your lifestyle?

Since I began my transition in early 2019, my life has changed dramatically and with incredible speed. Whether online with my social media, in my personal life, or as a businesswoman with global ambitions, ROMAN has evolved along with me as I finally engage with the world as the woman who has been waiting a lifetime to emerge. Alongside the clothes themselves, my relationship with the women who work for your company has been one of the highlights of this experience. To be accepted as one of them, to be treated as a VIP customer, to walk into the store and hear from the ladies that they saw my outfits on social media, to be part of a story in which we are all learning about acceptance of different perspectives and identities, to represent the transgender experience to a community that may not have had that much exposure to it....this is all incredibly meaningful to me personally.

Why ROMAN?

Your pieces are as dramatic and bold as my personality yet there is a class and an elegance to them that never feels anything less than high fashion. Every piece I've purchased feels like an investment that continues to pay dividends. The value for the cost is incredible. There is NOTHING in my closet from ROMAN that just hangs there - the pieces are timeless, infinitely wearable, and they have evolved along with me as I transition. I've had flings with other brands, but my love for ROMAN clothes is a relationship that I know will endure.

What's your go-to ROMAN USA piece?

Sheer pink wrap-around top. It is my go-to piece for making an unforgettable first impression. I wear it to first dates, I've featured it on my Instagram more than any other piece. It represents the perfect harmony of edgy and classy that I love about Roman clothes. My most memorable piece is the crushed velvet gown, because it is so over-the-top extra but in a way that I can pull off. I remember seeing it hanging in the store during my first time shopping there and thinking "There is NO WAY I will ever have the courage to try that on." And of course, as soon as I tried it on I had to have it.

Snapshot of an empowered Cassandra

Because of my appearance, my height, my features, my energy, etc., I am impossible to miss. I stand out in any crowd, especially now that we all have to stand six feet apart. I have embraced this boldness in every aspect of my life and it is the energy that I am tapping into to fuel the growth of my company, Graceful Change. ROMAN clothes allow me to express this unmistakable energy in a memorable way. The boldness and drama of your clothes are a pure expression of my own boldness and my own drama and serve as an immediate conversation-starter wherever I go, whoever I am working with. Whether as CEO of my company or out on a date or matching my outfit to a story I am sharing on my online platforms, ROMAN clothes empower me to express my authentic self in a way that I never have before.

Connection means so much to me and I feel very lucky to experience it here with so many authentic people from around the world. In particular, I adore those moments when I can be the Comment Fairy and sprinkle sincere love and appreciation for the beauty so many of you share.

Reciprocity is also a big deal to me. If you engage with my content I am honored to engage back. Even if it's a "OMG YUR SO HAWT" comment. At it's core that is a lovely sentiment and I appreciate it.

However...

Instagram often feels like a full time job— one that I enjoy very much!—but I know that I need to reduce my hours over the next couple weeks for both the launch of my business as well as, uh, #secretproject Part Two.

A very interesting opportunity has suddenly materialized, and it is something that I need to focus on with manic and relentless intensity. Like, burning fire of a thousand suns intensity.

So I ask you, my dear Instafamily, to wish me luck and to know that if I disappear for a bit from your feeds, that I consider that a sacrifice of something very meaningful to me. You might not notice, but I will.

I marvel at the endlessly inventive and creative ways so many of you share yourselves with the world. I am going to miss sharing my admiration for all your talents as much as I would like over the next few weeks.

See you soon!

#gratitude #nextlevel

#bigthingscoming #timetowork

#hustlehard #goodhairday

My first step in pulling this book together was to go back and look at all my content on Instagram. When I identified a post that I wanted to use, I copied its text into a Word file and then inserted the accompanying photo alongside it. The first time I did this I had a bit of a freak-out moment.

Unbeknownst to me, Word now has this feature where it automatically generates a description of the photo and includes it in a little banner along the bottom. Like, WTF kind of machine learning shenanigans are going on at my expense?

Aside from not wanting to accelerate Skynet's termination of the human race, though, there was another reason why this was freaking me out: what if HAL 9000 gets it wrong?

The very first description that our future AI overlords came up with was "A person in a striped shirt." Here we go, I'm thinking, I'm going to be called a dude in a dress by that fucking talking paperclip.

I move on to the next episode with nervous anticipation and Max Headroom describes it thusly: "A picture containing building, person, dress, person."

Now, there is a lot going on in my mind. My first thought is that we have much longer before the machines take over than I originally feared as they appear to be pretty stupid. Building? Oh yeah, right, because the doors look like bricks. Person twice? Get your vision checked, Clippy. But at least it got the dress right, so I breathe a sigh of relief.

And then it hits me: "OMG, the computer is perceiving the duality of my existence and is able to discern both the masculine and feminine identities on display." If this is the case, then we're screwed. Like, start unplugging stuff NOW!

Already thinking about how to keep posting on Instagram when I go off the grid, I move on to the next photo, which is the first Transition Tuesday side-by-side comparison that I posted.

Survey says: "Two people smiling for the camera."

This is the moment where I realize that the machines have already leapfrogged us in terms of rendering the gender binary obsolete. I am, however, a little concerned about whether or not Wall-E is going to make a good therapist. It looks at the photo on the left and sees someone smiling. I look at the photo on the left and see someone screaming on the inside, suffering immeasurable anguish, contemplating the pain and suffering that is making life unbearable.

Anyway, photo after photo was "person" this and "person" that and some of them were even kind of amusing. Here are a few of my favorites:

"A group of people standing in front of a crowd." This one made me laugh.

"A picture containing person, indoor, clothing, sitting." Damn straight that is clothing. Bubble Bath BIKINI, bitches!

"Two people dancing." This one is spot on. Rather deep. Perhaps there is hope for AI therapists after all.

"A picture containing young person standing." Ok, computer, you are trying to flatter me and I am not saying no to that.

"A picture containing graphical user interface." Now the computer finds me hot and wants to have sex. It was only a matter of time.

As far as what The Matrix saw in the photo accompanying this Epilogue, I am going to pull a surprise twist and refrain from additional commentary. I will merely say that like everything else in this book, what I am about to share actually happened. The significance of what this represents for my journey—my story—moves me to convulsive waves of grateful tears every time I contemplate it:

"A child taking a selfie"

*"We shall not cease from exploration
And the end of all our exploring
Will be to arrive where we started
And know the place for the first time."*

- T.S. Eliot

Acknowledgements

To my children, Lydia, Ben, and Nick, for the gift of your unconditional love, the freedom that you represent, and the many ways you all make the world a better place. You are exemplary human beings, my heroes, and I am blessed to have you in my life.

To Scott for being such a powerful Force for good and catalyst of change. You are an existential alchemist and I treasure our partnership.

To Grace for your vision, your tenacity, and your ambition. You held a mirror up so that I could better see myself, and in turn have helped me hold one up for others. #winwithgrace

To Mia for putting the "social" in social media, for being such a good pimp, and for teaching me volumes about female friendship.

To all the members of the Girl Gang from around the world who have welcomed me with open arms into their sorority.

To "Henry Cavill" for an infinite number of things, to include helping me apply all this creativity in a collaborative way.

And finally, to Henry Cavill for being so ridiculously smoking hot.

Grace Venes-Escaffi

Layout Designer | Photo Editor

Grace is a Peruvian-American creative professional based in McLean, Virginia. During her extended quarantine she founded The Escaffi Agency to help local businesses and non-profit organizations develop their brands, and designed the very literary masterpiece you just experienced. Grace enjoys Peruvian food, visiting Peru, and talking about Peru.

@gracevenescaffi | www.theescaffiagency.com

Nicole Morley

Lead Photo Editor

Nicole has her BFA in Photography from SVA and over 12 years experience in the photography industry. She currently works as a freelance photographer and digital retoucher, as well as running her own digital brand, Nicole in Colour, which focuses on inspiring feminine confidence through creativity and self love. Nicole lives in Connecticut and enjoys thrifting, chai tea, and cuddling with her fat cat.

@nicoleincolour | www.nicoleincolour.com

CASSANDRA GRACE WILL RETURN...

CPSIA information can be obtained
at www.ICGtesting.com
Printed in the USA
BVHW021745270421
605960BV00005B/189